# Kafka: A Study

# Kafka: A Study

*by*
ANTHONY THORLBY
*Professor of Comparative Literature*
*University of Sussex*

**ROWMAN AND LITTLEFIELD**
Totowa, New Jersey

ISBN 0–87471–121–5

© Anthony Thorlby 1972
First published in the U.S.A. 1972
by Rowman and Littlefield
Reprinted 1974

Printed in Great Britain

# Contents

Foreword     vi

Acknowledgements     vii

Biographical Note     ix

Chapter One: LIFE AND WORK     1

Chapter Two: THE SHORT STORIES     21

Chapter Three: THE NOVELS     52

Chapter Four: CONCLUSION: THE PROBLEM OF INTERPRETATION     84

Bibliography     100

# Foreword

This book is intended to help students of literature in schools and universities, as well as others who read Kafka for pleasure. As so many people have come to know and be fascinated by his work in English translation, all quotations in this book are given in English, although page references have been given to the German edition. For the most part the standard English translations have been used, but in some cases a new translation of a phrase or word is offered. Kafka makes much play with the multiple and metaphorical meanings of words, and adequate equivalents cannot always be found in another language. Some illustrations of this difficulty are given in the chapters that follow, and the German original has been included in such cases.

Kafka is of special interest to any student of modern literature in no matter what language. This is because he was so extraordinarily intelligent in his understanding of the generally unspoken assumptions that underlie many tendencies and techniques in modern writing – intelligent, that is, in self-understanding of his position as a writer.

A.K.T.
University of Sussex

# Acknowledgements

To acknowledge all that I have learnt from other scholars who have written about Kafka would be impossible. So much has been written about him that it is difficult even in the bibliography at the end to give anything like a fair selection of critical books; to have referred to other scholars' views in detail in the text would have taken up much space, which I have preferred to use for an analysis of Kafka's work that is, I hope, as original as can be expected at this already late stage in the debate. Sometimes my own view differs only slightly from that held by others; sometimes, however, it differs radically. I have indicated the main points of difference between my own and some earlier interpretations, though without attempting to refute the specific arguments of other scholars, many of which I have found valuable in arriving at my own conclusions.

I wish to thank S. Fischer Verlag and Schocken Books, New York, for permission to quote from the German edition of Kafka's work and to make translations from it, and Secker and Warburg for permission to quote from the English translations – and also to depart occasionally from these.

# Biographical Note

Franz Kafka was born on 3 July 1883, in Prague. He was the son of a successful, self-made merchant who had known hardship as a boy in the country. Both Kafka's father, Herrmann, and his mother Julie (*née* Löwy) were Jews; many of his family died as a result of Nazi persecution.

At university, Kafka studied literature briefly, then took up law in which he received his doctorate in 1906. He took a job with one insurance company, soon moved to another, the Arbeiter-Unfall-Versicherungs-Anstalt (Workers' Accident Insurance Company), with which he remained until he was pensioned off as a result of ill-health in 1922. His health was always weak, despite his persistent and even strenuous efforts to improve it; he visited several sanatoria, and died on 3 June 1924 in the Wienerwald Sanatorium in Vienna after suffering from tuberculosis first diagnosed seven years earlier.

Kafka passed almost all his life in Prague, making only short trips abroad and to the country, where he enjoyed particularly staying with his sister, Ottla, at Zürau. He several times made plans to marry, becoming officially engaged to Felice Bauer in 1914 and again in 1917; his last liaison was with Dora Dymant, with whom he lived for a while in Berlin in 1923, and who stayed with him till he died.

Only a small part of Kafka's writing was published during his lifetime, and he entrusted his unpublished works to Max Brod, his closest friend and a writer of some note, whom he asked to destroy them – although Max Brod had told him that he would not do so. Kafka remained relatively unknown until after the Second World War (for notorious reasons in the German-speaking world), but since then he has gained an international reputation as one of the greatest writers of the twentieth century.

# 1

# Life and Work

## Kafka's extraordinary achievement, and aims, as a writer

Karl Kraus, wno was Kafka's contemporary and also a citizen of the Austro-Hungarian Empire in its last decades, once wrote: 'The understanding of my work is made more difficult by a knowledge of my material.' The same is true of Franz Kafka. Editors, critics, and biographers have made available every scrap of information, every traceable manuscript, even remarks remembered by other people, that might throw light on Kafka's fiction. It cannot be said that all this material has helped very much – and yet it is in a certain sense indispensable. The sense in which it is helpful is largely a negative one: it makes clear the extent to which Kafka has made the autobiographical element in his work unrecognizable. But, of course, we need to know something about what he and his life were actually like in order to recognize how strangely both have become transformed in his writing.

Whether it is *permissible* that Kafka's life, and particularly his inner life, his fantasy world from which he drew his inspiration, should be pried into, is another question. Kafka asked his close friend, the novelist and critic Max Brod, to destroy his unpublished manuscripts. Max Brod did not comply, for reasons that he explained in a postscript to one of the novels of Kafka's that he published posthumously (*The Trial*). Had he complied, we should possess now only a handful of stories, and it is unlikely that Kafka would have achieved the kind of international fame that has been accorded to him since the Second World War. The letters Kafka wrote, especially those to the women who meant most to him, Felice Bauer and Milena Jesenská, might still have come to light. Some material and – what is incomparably more tragic – many persons related to Kafka's existence have perished without trace as a result of Nazi persecution of the Jews. It is in these exceptional circumstances, both intimately personal and globally political, that the question arises of what is the 'right' way to understand Kafka.

Suppression and oppression are part of the process that has made Kafka famous. His prose narratives contain to a unique degree symbolic statements of what civilized men have had to suffer in this century. These statements are not realistic descriptions of persecution in modern society. Kafka's fiction is not realistic in the normal sense of that word, and his own interest in politics and social conditions was, as regards his writing, very slight. The problem that has prompted so many critics to write more about Kafka than about any other writer since the war is this: how has it come about that an author so apparently indifferent to the world about him, so apparently turned in on himself, should have symbolized so profoundly events that occurred, and were increasingly to occur, outside his own experience and above all after his death? The English language even looks like accepting as an adjective, having a meaning familiar to a considerable number of people, the word 'Kafkaesque' (a distinction conferred for a while on the name of Shaw, and more lastingly on that of Dickens). The answer to the problem raised by Kafka's work has indeed a lot to do with what words mean, and particularly with the different kinds of meaning they can have – including, as we shall see, the dreadful possibility that they have no ultimately reliable meaning at all.

In saying this, we meet again the same kind of paradox that we mentioned at the start. In order to recognize an ultimate inadequacy in language, we must have something to compare it with. We need to be able to see that words seem to mean some-

thing at one level that at another level they do not. In real life
we may often feel that words are inadequate; in some cases
other forms of objective verification may be used to check their
correctness. But if a writer wants to make clear in words the inadequacy of words, he faces a peculiarly difficult task. For he
has both to evoke their meaning and to suppress it at the same
time. This is one way of describing Kafka's literary technique.
He presents a story, often no more than a simple incident or
situation, which has an apparently realistic, surface meaning.
As we look at it, however, we seem to see through it, as though
it were also unreal, weird, nightmarish. We cannot then say for
sure what other meaning we have glimpsed, and as a result
*positive* interpretations of Kafka's symbolism have provoked
wide disagreement amongst critics. Perhaps the only point of
agreement is that Kafka's fiction cannot be taken at its face
value and read like conventional novels about the real world.
Realist writers generally want to make us believe in and understand the world as they describe it. Kafka wants to do this too,
of course, since he too is a writer; but he also wants to do the
opposite – to make us aware that the reality before us is in-
credible and incomprehensible.

Kafka knew well enough how paradoxical his aim and
method as a writer were. He recalled and recorded in later
years his ambitions as a young man:

> [I was sitting once] thinking over the things I wanted in
> life. What seemed most important and attractive was the
> wish to achieve a view of life (and – necessarily connected
> with this, of course – to be able to make other people
> believe in it by writing), in which life would still preserve
> its natural, solid course of ups and downs, but at the same
> time would be seen just as clearly to be a nothing, a dream,
> a weightless movement. A good wish perhaps, if I had
> desired it aright. Rather like wishing to hammer a table
> together with painstaking care and skill and at the same
> time to be doing nothing; and not in such a way that
> people could say: 'He doesn't take hammering seriously',

> but so that they would say: 'When he hammers he really means it but it is also nothing to him.' And the act of hammering would thereby have become still more daring, more determined, more real, and also perhaps more mad.
> (*Beschreibung eines Kampfes*, pp. 293 f)

This passage illustrates the way Kafka's creative intelligence works. He is, as the opening sentences make clear, talking about the art of writing, which will make the real world both real and unreal, a 'nothing' (*ein Nichts*). In order to grasp what kind of activity his writing will be, he chooses a simile, likening it to carpentry. Immediately a scene takes shape before his eyes, with people speaking, commenting upon his 'work'. This projection outwards of a mental activity, that transforms it into an apparently concrete job in real surroundings, makes his work both more serious and more mad. In the next sentence Kafka refers to himself no longer as 'I' but as 'he':

> But he could not wish any such thing, for his wish was no wish at all, it was merely a defence, a civilizing of nothingness (*Nichts*), a touch of lovely humour that he wanted to bestow on that nothingness, where he had only just begun to consciously take his first few steps, but which he already felt to be his element. (ibid., p. 294)

We see here Kafka's ability to turn his self-reflections into a concrete symbol, indeed into a whole symbolic world where things and people take on an objective reality – so that 'I' becomes 'he' – *and also* to stand back and observe the impossibility of the task. This constitutes the essence of Kafka's genius. In the language of existentialism, with which Kafka is sometimes associated, it constitutes an exercise in self-alienation. The obscure depths of meaning that are suggested by Kafka's symbolism are empty or negative depths; their psychological secret is the discovery of nothingness. The 'view of life' Kafka wished to achieve was and is a nihilistic viewpoint. His fiction will seem true to us in so far as we share it, that is to say, in so far as we see the world from out of empty

space. Kafka's positive lesson is that he teaches us just where
we may be standing and looking from, and what are the consequences of this nihilistic position. He wrote a number of
aphorisms about the figure called 'he', in which he observes his
position as observer. One of them is as follows:

> He has found the Archimedean point, but has used it
> against himself; evidently this is the condition that has
> enabled him to find it.
> (In *Hochzeitsvorbereitungen auf dem Lande*, p. 418)

## Kafka's cultural and social background

The two-sidedness of Kafka's talent, which has produced a
truly profound ambiguity in his writing (apart from simple disagreement amongst his critics), can be related to his situation as
a Jewish writer in Prague at the beginning of this century. This
is not to suggest that Kafka's gift for bestowing more than just
'a touch of lively humour' on nothingness, his combination of
subtle intelligence and deep moral, even religious feeling, is not
unique and personal in degree. But in kind there is something
typical about it. Kafka was born into a distinctive social and
cultural milieu that provided him with remarkable spiritual re-
sources.

It is important to recall, for instance, how greatly Jewish
intellectual life had been retarded in Europe, partly as a result
of social constraints imposed from without and amounting at
times to violent persecution, and partly as a result of a deeply
conservative vein within the Jewish religious tradition itself.
Kafka was born at a time and place where the possibility, and
therefore the problem, of assimilation into non-Jewish society
was still recent and acute (severely restrictive laws were in force
against the Jews in the Hapsburg Empire until 1848, as regards
such matters as residence, employment, marriage, and above
all, education). Kafka's father was a self-made man from the
country, and one of the steps he took to gain success in Prague

was to adopt German as his language and hence make it the language of his family. This further complicated the situation of his sensitive son, Franz, who grew up to find himself speaking the language of an influential, largely upper-class minority.

Kafka himself never suffered any persecution, but he was inwardly unsure about whether he 'belonged' in the society in which he lived. Even without the complications of his Czech and Jewish background, it is likely that Kafka would have experienced this doubt in some form, for it had been growing into a major obsession amongst writers for over a century, ever since the first romantic moan about the poet's solitude had sounded so effective. Kafka's situation as a German-speaking Jew in Prague gave him fresher and deeper access to this no longer new source of inspiration.

With Kafka it was not a case of feeling spiritually superior to an unfeeling, ugly, or materialistic world. He was not interested so much in the inadequacies of the society from which he felt alienated as in the complexities of his own state of mind. Far from producing books that imply the world is at fault for failing to satisfy human expectations (as rather too many simple-minded books of recent times have done), Kafka meditated critically upon these expectations themselves. In his fiction it is not clear who or what is at fault. Critics have brought social, religious, and psychological explanations in, to show what Kafka 'really' meant. But as we have said, he is not a realist writer; he himself was not looking for some external frame of reference to which to refer the question of what existence 'means', and it seems somewhat inappropriate for critics to try and provide him with one.

What did fascinate Kafka was the possibility of finding an internal way of grasping the meaning of meaning (which in his case meant the meaning of writing, the meaning of words). If he could do this, he would be free of all the uncertainties that surround any fixed frame of reference. And we should note that a longing for freedom is the other face of the condition of solitude in Kafka's fiction; it is likewise rooted in his experience of being a writer.

The difference made by his being a Jewish writer can again be described as a problem of assimilation. Let us take, by way of contrast to Kafka's preoccupation with the meaning of meaning, a common-sense realist view of the question. If meaning is not accepted as referring to a context of experience or rules outside itself, the question could be said to fall into an infinite recession. (Once this type of question is accepted as itself meaningful, you can go on to ask: 'What is the meaning of the meaning of meaning?' And so on.) What may be described as an 'assimilated' mind will then feel justified in putting a stop to this type of inquiry, which clearly leads nowhere.

Kafka, as we have seen, was under no illusion about the fact that his destination, his 'element', was nowhere, *das Nichts*. But this in no way weakened his determination to go on, just as K. goes on towards the unattainable castle, where there await him, even if he got there, unimaginable hierarchies of 'authority', an infinite recession of 'trials' from which he will never be set free. The fact that Kafka could not, as it were, leave well alone and simply live in the world without asking such impossible questions is due to his having the sensibility not only of a writer but of a Jewish writer. No writer of any intelligence can be fully assimilated to his earthly condition, the condition of having a mortal mind. A Jewish writer is likely to feel doubly unassimilated, because the roots of his mental life reach back into soil that is quite different from that on which the traditions of Western reason and common sense have been erected. It is religious soil, and three things must be said about it that are relevant to Kafka.

First, Judaism is an essentially different kind of religion from Christianity. This is not simply because of the explicitly new departure recorded in the Gospels (a matter that is not relevant here), but because of the long centuries of effort on the part of the Christian church to assimilate religious truth to the truths of reason as these were inherited independently in the West from the Greco-Roman world. This process of assimilation reached its apogee in the late eighteenth and early nineteenth century, passing over into modes of thinking from which the religious element was fast disappearing, being replaced by increasingly materialist and scientific conceptions of man's destiny.

This point was reached, therefore, at about the same time as Jewish emancipation began so very belatedly to take place in Europe. One result of this was that a Jewish intellectual was potentially endowed with a remarkable spiritual constitution and opportunity: one part of his mind might still be close to an archaic, unassimilated religious tradition, while another part found the sophisticated intellectual equipment of modernity at his disposal. In Kafka's case, we find a familiar form of modern rationality expressing itself, challenging the world with a typical mixture of religious scepticism, moral idealism, and egotistical determination; but we also find a deeper resonance behind this plausible surface – the resonance of a religious seriousness that lacks any positively religious commitment. We may say that Kafka believes in nothing, but feels that the condition of believing in nothing is dreadful.

Here a second point needs to be made, concerning precisely this word 'dread'. The insight that reason may not be assimilable to existence has by no means been the exclusive prerogative of Jewish thinkers; it has been the starting point for that type of philosophizing known generally as existentialism, and was the starting point in particular for the Danish theological writer, Søren Kierkegaard. Now, Kafka read some of Kierkegaard's work, recognizing how deeply it touched his own condition, and responding most evidently to his forerunner's 'Concept of Dread'.

Dread or *Angst*, as it has come almost internationally to be called, is perhaps the only significant discovery of a new component of the psyche in modern times, something between an emotion and a thought, and yet not classifiable under the conventional categories of earlier psychology. It is the experience evoked in a man by the awareness of his selfhood and of the infinite discrepancy between what he knows and what he is. It is the experience that is symbolized and to some extent communicated by Kafka's writing. Kafka approached this abyss of uncertainty from a background unlike that of Kierkegaard, who was after all a Christian apologist. But their psychological discovery is similar in that it springs from a confrontation between a modern self-conscious intelligence and the *mysterium tremendens* of temporal existence.

The third aspect of Kafka's Jewishness that requires comment can only be sketched here in barest outline. It concerns the association of ordinary, everyday existence in time with a mystery of religious, or in some other way spiritually binding, importance. The tendency of Christian theology was for centuries, as we have said, to identify things divine with universal principles of morality and truth that stood above the realm of time and change. The Judaic religion has remained more firmly grounded in historical lore; and it resembles less an ideology, in the sense of premises and arguments to be understood, than a way of life, a ritual established on the authority of precedent and custom. This is not to deny that the Talmud offers commentary, interpretation, and analysis in plenty; but the subtlety of Rabbinical intelligence (and humour) has lain rather in adjusting thought to the decrees of the inscrutable.

Kafka was not well informed about his own religion, and his feelings towards it were ambivalent; at various stages in his life he became deeply impressed by some aspect of Judaism – by the Zionist movement, for instance, by Hassidic literature, and on one occasion by a troupe of Yiddish actors. But it is not here that we find the most telling marks of Kafka's racial religion upon his writing (however many putative similarities, borrowings, and influences critics knowledgeable in Jewish lore may detect in Kafka's work). We find them rather in the 'faith-value', to quote Kafka's own term, that he sensed in the simple act of living. It is characteristic of Kafka that we find this expression not in a personal profession of faith but in an aphoristic dialogue, which is an extremely detached literary form – and a favourite one for telling Jewish jokes:

> 'It cannot be said that we are lacking in faith. Even the simple fact of our life is of a faith-value that can never be exhausted.' 'You suggest there is some faith-value in this? One *cannot* not live, after all.' 'It is precisely in this "cannot, after all" that the mad strength of faith lies; it is in this negation that it takes on form.'
> (In *Hochzeitsvorbereitungen auf dem Lande*, Aphorism 109, p. 54)

One other example may be quoted, this time from a letter to Max Brod. It shows again the kind of spiritual fascination aroused in Kafka by the appearance of security, of confident belonging, that he saw *in other people*:

> When I opened my eyes after a short afternoon nap . . . I heard my mother speaking to someone from the balcony and asking them in a quite natural way: 'What are you doing?' A woman answered from the garden: 'I am having tea on the lawn.' And I was amazed at the assurance (*Festigkeit*) with which people are able to bear life.
> (*Briefe 1902–1924*, p. 29)

### Freudian Neurosis

Kafka's own life was outwardly ordinary and secure enough – compared, for instance, with the Bohemian existence of many European artists and writers – but he never felt inwardly at home in it. Yet he lived in his family's home for many years, worked full-time in an insurance office most of his life, and repeatedly made plans to get married and settle down. His attempts and failure to achieve this latter goal constituted the one, long, complex adventure of his inner world, where it was inextricably bound up with his inspiration as a writer.

As we might expect with Kafka, the connection is both very clear and profoundly obscure, resembling almost a form of self-torture he could not do without. It certainly resembles the psychological state that Kafka's great contemporary, Sigmund Freud (whose early work he knew about), was in these same years defining as neurotic. Kafka even reached, independently of Freud, the same conclusion that the origin of such neurosis lies in a son's relationship to his father. At the age of thirty-six Kafka wrote a 'letter' to his father – which he never delivered – that is a small masterpiece of psychoanalytic writing. If Freud's theory of analytical self-understanding is true, then Kafka's astonishing clearsightedness, in which there appears to be no trace of repression or fantasy, should signify that he was cured. Indeed, at one point in his 'letter to his father'* Kafka describes all his writing as a form of psychoanalytic cure: 'a long-drawn-out leave-taking from you', he says to his father: and again: 'My writing was all about you.' Whenever some stories of his had been published and he presented a copy to his father, not even his father's indifference could prevent Kafka from feeling – and as he subtly observes, perhaps helped him to feel – 'Now you are free.'

Did Kafka's writing, did the self-knowledge displayed not only in this letter to his father but in so many other letters and journal jottings, set him free? Kafka himself goes on: 'Of course, it was a delusion; I was not, or, to put it most optimistically, I was not *yet* free.' Of his writing, perhaps of this letter, perhaps of all his books, he remarks: 'How little all this amounted to!' The ambiguity about what 'this' refers to increases in the following sentence, where Kafka says that 'in my childhood it ruled my life as a premonition, later as a hope, and still later often as despair, dictating – it may be said, yet again in your shape – my few little decisions to me'. What is this 'it' which ruled Kafka's life 'in the shape of' his father?

* Also printed posthumously in the volume entitled *Hochzeitsvorbereitungen auf dem Lande und andere Prosa aus dem Nachlaß*.

Freud too resorted to the same word, the *id*, to describe the force that ultimately rules men's lives, expressing itself through various channels and 'shapes', some of them seeming – according largely to local customs – more healthy or normal than others. Can any man be entirely free of 'it', unless he dies? And the very desire to be free: is that perhaps merely another expression of 'it', only disguised in some peculiarly fatal and self-destructive form? Is the life instinct ultimately inseparable, perhaps even indistinguishable, from a death instinct?

These are all questions that cannot be answered within the frame of reference constructed by modern psychology. Kafka knew as well as any psychoanalyst to what remote depths, inaccessible to the light of consciousness, all the processes of the mind may be referred. And he knew more; he knew that no certain, scientific knowledge can ever unlock the labyrinthine secrets of the soul, the truly crucial secrets of 'conscience' in the sense not merely of man's capacity to feel guilt but of all his closely related capacities for self-awareness, for knowledge, for creative aspiration towards freedom and truth and beauty. The mind cannot unlock its own secrets, because the more highly rationalistic, conceptual, and verbally precise its questioning becomes, the more inappropriate it is to the 'thing' it is asking about. The modern manner of handling life intellectually – and Kafka had a pre-eminently modern intelligence – makes the thing impossible to grasp. The mysterious origins of the spirit recede into the impenetrable murk of something that looks absurd, obscene, and even evil. No wonder that Kafka should once have noted down despairingly: 'Never again any psychology!'

The hope of cure, of being set free, which sustains Kafka's writing, remains inseparable from his sense of enslavement, his manifest neurosis, which (in his own eyes at least) reached psychosomatic proportions. He repeatedly interpreted the tuberculosis that finally caused his death as a self-inflicted wound. Writing again to Max Brod about his desire for 'freedom, freedom above all else', he goes on in characteristically ambiguous terms: 'Admittedly the wound is still here, of which my sick lung is only the symbol.' Where is 'here'? In the desire for freedom? In the village where he happened then to be staying with his favourite sister, Ottla? Or simply in life itself, where the nameable diseases that kill us are only symbols of an inescapable, inscrutable decree that all men must die?

In Genesis a story is told of why men have to die: because Adam was beguiled through Eve into wanting knowledge of good and evil. Kafka often meditated upon this Biblical story, and upon other mythological stories that symbolize the human condition. For such stories do enable us to grasp life as a whole, and (if we believe in them) to have faith in life's ultimate meaningfulness – even though the myth may be an account of how we come to be deprived of that meaningful life which would be Paradise. Kafka's own writing has a similar mythological quality, in that his imagination conceives symbolic stories of man's deprived spiritual state. His myths symbolize the ills of modern selfconsciousness, the self-destructive urge to know oneself, assert one's innocence and rights, and through knowledge and determination to achieve freedom.

Kafka's myths differ from those of ancient tradition, however, as he well knew. For those of tradition (whether classical or Judaic) are based on a belief in the reality of the gods, that is to say, in the objective reality of spiritual forces external to men, of spiritual values embodied *in* the world. Kafka's modern, sceptical intelligence did not allow him to believe this. His myths, like his seemingly religious attitude towards his writing, point not outwards towards the world but inwards against himself.

### Kafka's 'philosophy'

Kafka's mythology, then, is based not on observation of the world but on observation of the self. His extraordinarily subtle insight into this process does not constitute a psychology, in the sense that it illumines worldly passions such as love, jealousy, greed and the like. Kafka's imagination reaches beyond all particular contents of the self to form mythological pictures of the total process of self-consciousness. And he encounters, as a result, the inevitable limit of all efforts at total understanding, where words pass over into symbols whose meaning cannot be related to anything beyond themselves.

His symbols resemble a second myth of the Fall, with the difference that they are not set in the context of a God-created paradise man has lost, but of a man-made hell he cannot escape from. Apart from the stories that symbolize this situation, Kafka's notebooks contain many aphoristic speculations, which formulate it abstractly; they provide a kind of inverted theology to explain the inverted myths of his fiction. He writes, for instance:

> The observer of the soul cannot penetrate into the soul, but there doubtless is a margin where he comes into contact with it. Recognition of this contact is the fact that even the soul does not know itself. Hence it must remain unknown. That would be sad only if there were anything apart from the soul, but there is nothing else.
>
> (In *Hochzeitsvorbereitungen*, p. 93)

Kafka often repeats the assertion, which on the face of it seems highly improbable, but which forms a major premise of his 'theology' and is essential to an understanding of his fiction, that 'there is nothing besides a spiritual world'. Whatever reaction this may provoke in readers brought up in a more realistic tradition, it must constantly be remembered that Kafka found his inspiration by immersing himself totally in his mental world and trying to describe his 'dream-like inner life'. The conflicts that produce such suffering and despair in his stories have not been conceived in the rationally objective manner of most conventional writing, i.e. as conflicts between real persons or (what conventionally has been supposed to be at the base of these) as a conflict between man's bodily and his spiritual nature. The division within Kafka's world is a division of the mind against itself.

The spiritual character of Kafka's world is seen again in the following notes, which pass with a sudden and, at first sight, mysterious jump to a moral speculation, where one might not have expected there to be any grounds for moral judgements of any kind:

> Three different things:
> Looking on oneself as something alien, forgetting the sight, remembering the gaze.
> Or only two different things, for the third includes the second.
> Evil is the starry sky of the Good.
>
> (In *Hochzeitsvorbereitungen*, p. 90)

The starry sky, traditional symbol of Heaven, has become for Kafka a symbol of the opposite, of evil. What does this inversion mean? First, let us remark that Kafka often says similar things about evil, even though his symbolism varies. For instance, the phrase quoted above to the effect that: 'There is nothing besides a spiritual world', continues as follows:

> What we call the world of the senses is the evil in the spiritual world, and what we call evil is only a necessity of a moment in our eternal evolution.
>
> (ibid., Aphorism 54, p. 44)

Or again:

> Evil is a radiation of the human consciousness in certain transitional positions. It is not actually the sensual world that is a mere appearance, what is so is the evil of it, which, admittedly, is what constitutes the sensual world in our eyes.     (ibid., Aphorism 85, pp. 49 and 102)

Kafka's next aphorism then concludes:

> . . . the whole visible world is perhaps nothing other than a motivation of man's wish to rest for a moment – an

attempt to falsify the fact of knowledge, to try to turn the
knowledge into the goal.

(ibid., Aphorism 86, pp. 49 and 103)

Evil, then, is for Kafka attributable in some way to human
consciousness; it is a kind of mistake or failure within the
evolutionary process of the mind. It seems to come about from
the mind's desire not to evolve further, 'to rest for a moment',
and to accept as final, as real, its knowledge of the world.

Since Kafka's time, the spread of existentialist philosophies
has made more familiar such assumptions as these: that the
world has no fixed reality, that existence is something which is
eternally being created within human consciousness, and that
the only evil is to deny this creative role and try to 'rest' with
the fixity of appearances. Kafka himself could have become
familiar with such assumptions through his reading of Kierkegaard, or through his knowledge of Nietzsche. The weakness of
existentialist thinking, just as much in Kierkegaard as in
Nietzsche, and apparent again in Heidegger and Sartre, lies in
the difficulty of establishing any valid morality, i.e. one having
regard to the good of other persons or any real results in the
world. To the existentialist mind, *whatever* one does (or thinks)
will, as soon as it is embarked on and starts to become real, also
start to appear wrong – or 'evil', in Kafka's phrase.

The redeeming feature of Kafka's inverted theology as far as
his writing is concerned is that he was obviously aware of the
fatal paradox embedded in it. 'The state in which we are is
sinful, irrespective of guilt,' he writes; and in the same vein:
'The fact that there is nothing but a spiritual world deprives us
of hope and gives us certainty.' (Aphorisms 83 and 62) As we
have suggested, Kafka's ability to pronounce upon the predicament of the modern intelligence, and above all to symbolize
this in stories that have religious profundity and the archaic
surrealism of myth, may have been due to a still deeply Jewish
feeling for the God-ordained character of life. Aphorism 83
begins by declaring: 'We are sinful not only because we have

eaten of the Tree of Knowledge, but also because we have not yet eaten of the Tree of Life.'

Kafka's conception of the sanctity of life, in contrast to which he saw the starry heaven of self-observing thought as evil, is quite distinct from the *avant-garde* cults of sex, vitalism, and the like, which were fashionable in his day. His values in this respect sound quite piously conventional. He writes to his father:

> Marrying, founding a family, accepting all the children that come, supporting them in this insecure world and even guiding them a little as well, is, I am convinced the utmost a human being can succeed in doing at all.
>
> (ibid., p. 209)

But as he wrote to the sister of another girl – Julie Wohryzek – with whom he broke off his engagement; 'We were both perfectly clear that I regarded marriage and children as in a certain sense the highest thing to be striven for on earth, but that I was quite incapable of getting married.' Doubtless it was from this incapacity, this betrayal of the highest good on earth, that Kafka's sense of guilt largely sprang; but so also did his inspiration as a writer.

## Conclusion

In conclusion, then, we may sum up the paradoxical relationship of Kafka's work to his life as follows: his fiction is not 'about' his life in any conventional sense, and yet it *is* a symbolic expression of his life to an unusually intimate and intense degree. To pore over the letters Kafka wrote to Felice Bauer, with whom he twice became engaged but never married, can tell a reader of *The Trial* little of interest above the level of indiscreet gossip, and may actually mislead him. For the one important fact that detailed knowledge of Kafka's unhappy love life is liable to obscure is this: novels like *The Trial*, or stories like *The Judgement*, which have some psychological connection with Kafka's affairs with other people, are not recognizably about those affairs. More important still, they are not about human affairs *of that kind*. That is to say, they are not descriptions of the kind of events that we (or Kafka) could observe in the world, with merely some of the details changed or invented.

The course of events in Kafka's fiction (i.e. the plot), together with the way the personages react (i.e. their character), are frequently trivial or incomprehensible when judged by common-sense standards of realism. A critic who tries to work out the connection between, say, Frieda (in *The Castle*) and Milena Jesenská, or Klamm and Ernst Polak (Milena's husband), is going in the wrong direction and undoing Kafka's intellectual work.

Kafka's work aims at understanding its own inward character, not that of other people. And we must stress again that it is the inward character of his life as a writer that he strives to understand. Kafka is not *describing* even his own life in its outward aspect, as so many writers have done with more or less exaggeration during the last two hundred years. He made a new departure in the already well-established business of ego-gazing that is based on a quite radical realization: namely, that one cannot know oneself in the same way that one knows things and people outside oneself. Thus he writes:

> How pathetically scanty my self knowledge is compared with, say, my knowledge of my room ... Why? There is no such thing as observation of the inner world, as there is of the outer world. At least descriptive psychology is probably, taken as a whole, a form of anthropomorphism, a nibbling* at our own limits. The inner world can only be experienced, not described.           (ibid., p. 72)

Similarly, it makes not much sense of *The Castle* to assume that it is a satire on bureaucracy based upon Kafka's experience as an employee of an insurance company. Not only do large

* The German text has 'ein Ausragen der Grenzen', but the incorrect English translation still conveys Kafka's meaning.

chunks of the text become irrelevant or boring on this assumption, but the attitudes and experiences of the hero seem in detail inexplicable and inappropriate. Of course, there is plenty of evidence to show that Kafka found his job ever more frustrating and irksome. 'My job is unbearable to me,' he wrote to Max Brod, 'because it contradicts my sole desire and my only vocation, which is literature. As I am nothing but literature, and neither can nor want to be anything else, my job can never have any hold over me, though it certainly can shatter me completely.' The whole point of *The Castle* is that K., the hero, wants to reach, enter, and master some organization that has an immense hold over him – and not simply a material hold such as jobs have over anyone who has to earn his living.

K. would seem both in *The Trial* and *The Castle* to be in a position merely to ignore the mysterious 'authorities' if he wanted to. Again, the point is that K. does not want to; the authorities fascinate him and he is drawn to them with his whole being. And as the letter to Max Brod says, his whole being is literature; it is literature that draws Kafka to itself, and to the impenetrably guilty and locked – the German word for 'castle' (*Schloß*) also means 'lock' – recesses of himself. Kafka's satire (if that is the right word for his style of writing) is directed against the impossibilities and immoralities not of any organization in society but of the sources of 'authority' in his, an author's, mind.

As we have seen, his intellectual assessment of what he wanted his writing to achieve was ambiguous: he wanted it to achieve everything and nothing – and he thought that the predicament of self-knowledge was typified by this problem. Kafka's moral assessment of the situation is even more vividly divided. We sometimes find him expressing the hope that his writing will be able to 'raise the world up into [a state of] purity, truth, and immutability'. More frequently we find descriptions of his enterprise that reveal both to what spiritual victory it aspired and to what dangers he was exposed:

One can disintegrate the world by means of very strong light. For weak eyes the world becomes solid, for still weaker eyes it seems to develop fists, for eyes weaker still it becomes shamefaced and smashes anyone who dares to gaze upon it.*                                    (ibid., p. 91)

At the other end of the scale, however, we find Kafka judging writing in the harshest terms:

Writing is a sweet and marvellous reward – but for what? Last night it came home to me with the clarity of an object lesson for children, that it is the reward for serving the devil. This descent to the dark powers, this setting free of spirits that nature meant to be held in check, questionable embracings and all the rest of it that is probably going on deep down, which one doesn't know about any more if one writes stories by the light of day. Perhaps there is another way of writing, but the only one I know is this: at night, when I cannot sleep for *Angst* – that is the only sort of writing I know. And it seems to me quite clear why it is devilish. It is the vanity and pleasure-seeking practice of whirling around one's own person all the time, or around someone else's – the movement then reduplicates itself, producing a solar system of vanity –, and of enjoying them. The thing an ordinary, simple man sometimes wishes: 'I'd like to die and see how people are sorry that I've gone,' is what a writer actually keeps doing; he dies (or doesn't really live) and is perpetually sorry for himself.
                              (Letter to Max Brod, July 1922)

* The ambiguity in this aphorism lies in the suggestion that Kafka both aspired to possess the very strong light and yet knew what it was like to suffer (spiritually) from very weak eyes. The difficulty introduced into his writing by his playing opposite roles simultaneously will be discussed further in the next chapter.

# 2

# The Short Stories

Myths are essentially short. They can be elaborated, of course, and be told in a sophisticated style, and be added to and varied; but all these elaborations and embellishments do not add anything of *mythological* interest to the original, simple story.

The mythological character of Kafka's imagination shows in his gift for conceiving a situation, a scene, sometimes a single image, that is replete with significance. These Kafkaesque situations 'speak worlds', as it were, and nothing that is said afterwards alters the essential shape of any of these worlds, no matter how much detail is added. Indeed, the reader may as a result have the impression that he is getting nowhere as he presses on through the unfinished chapters of *The Castle*, and wonder whether Kafka ever could have written a conclusion that would have put the hero into any position that he was not already in at the start. Certainly a reader who expects, from his experience of more conventional novels or of the drama, that the plot and the characters should develop in some necessary way, is likely to be uneasy at the thought that there could ever be serious uncertainty about the order in which Kafka intended to place the chapters he completed for *The Trial*, or about whether he might have written one or two more.

All in all, we may not be surprised if the verdict of posterity is that Kafka is at his best as a short-story writer, however valuable the novels may have been in establishing his fame (it could be argued that their power also rests at bottom on the simple situation from which they spring). The simple situation

that Kafka's imagination repeatedly tries to grasp as a whole is
the point where two incompatible, incommensurable things
meet and conflict. What the two things are can only be stated
symbolically, not realistically. For a realistic view implies that
we are able to look on at the conflicting parties from outside.
If, however, the conflict that Kafka is trying to imagine is the
total one of the mind's situation in the world, there is clearly no
outside position, in any realistic sense, from which he can look
on. In Kafka's fiction we can usually not be sure (i.e. in terms
of a realistic interpretation) what his symbols 'mean', in the
sense of 'refer to'. But we can always see quite clearly that there
is tension and conflict. Even his notebook jottings have this
clarity, right down to a short sentence, such as: 'A shout arises
out of a river' or even the single compound word: 'Pigsticking'.

## Beschreibung eines Kampfes ('Description of a Fight', 1904/5)*

Since there is no space to discuss all of Kafka's stories in detail,
and enough general remarks about his work have now been
made, the best course will be to look at a few of the stories as
closely as possible, beginning with the earliest, 'Description of
a Fight'. This is already a characteristic piece of Kafkaesque
writing, in that it exists in more than one version, consists of
vivid scenes that are strung together in no necessary order, and
is unfinished. The fight takes place between two characters who
are referred to simply as 'I' and 'he', and who have, by conventional standards, few memorable characteristics. For all
that, their struggle is real and intense, and it occurs in a frozen
landscape that is partly a recognizable part of Prague – it must
be the Laurenziberg, which was the scene of Kafka's youthful
meditations on his life's ambition (recorded above, pp. 3–4) –

* The dates given in parentheses after each title indicate when the work
was written.

and is partly a fantasy landscape that one or both of the characters enter at various stages in the story.

This mixture of realism and fantasy is not always successful here, but it is typical of Kafka's style, which at its best produces an indissoluble fusion of the two, so that the reader begins to accept nightmarish absurdities as matters of fact. Where the style is uneven, as it is in 'Description of a Fight' and continues to be still in a later book like *America* (1912), the characters and environment appear now in one light, now in another: at one moment there is normal conversation in a bar, at another weird, dreamlike behaviour in forests and deserted squares.

Both 'I' and 'he' represent aspects of Kafka himself, but again it is difficult to define them; the only thing that is clearly defined is the rift and tension between them, the fact that Kafka is divided against himself. 'He', for instance, is probably not the intellectually detached 'he' of the aphorisms, who had reached the Archimedean point. This 'he' is a man involved in a love affair which 'I' feels called upon to sort out. 'I', in fact, rides on the back of 'he', whom he brings at the end to stab himself – an uncanny anticipation of the idea of a self-inflicted wound which was to recur to Kafka's mind when tuberculosis 'released' him from his obligation to marry. 'I' would seem, therefore, to be playing the role here of Kafka's intellectual self.

'I's' relationship to the 'he' who lives in society and falls in love becomes particularly understandable in this light in the scene where 'he' goes through the outward motions of prayer rather too ostentatiously and is criticized for being bogus – or inauthentic, in the language of more recent existentialism – by the critical, uncommitted 'I'. 'He' answers that he has to pray in public like this, because he needs the gaze of other people in order to feel himself 'hammered together'. We have already quoted Kafka's use of this striking image in connection with his own writing, where the hammering was to be taken with complete seriousness and yet to mean nothing at all. It is likely that this crucial image of the section entitled 'Conversation with the Praying Man', which Kafka published as a separate story (in *Hyperion*, March–April 1909), was important to Kafka less as a realistic psychological insight into the way any man actually prays than as a symbol of the relationship between reality and writing with which he personally was so deeply concerned.

If we look at the story, 'Conversation with a Praying Man', on its own, however, we find that the definition of the roles played by 'I' and 'he' is not entirely consistent with what has been said above, and might even be said to be the other way round. For instance, it is 'he' who tells the anecdote of the woman calling out that she is having tea on the lawn (quoted above, p. 10, from a letter of Kafka's to Max Brod); and it is 'he' who finds it extraordinary, and 'I' who protests that it is not. 'I' plays the part rather of a rational psychoanalyst who knows what the experiences of 'he' are like: they suggest 'he' is in a state of existential 'nausea' – Kafka actually used words similar to those employed by Kierkegaard to describe dread, though he had not then read Kierkegaard, and similar to those made famous since by Sartre – and 'I' is the one anxious that 'he' should conquer it.

The story concludes by 'he' making flattering remarks about 'I's' worldly appearance and suggesting that 'confessions become most clear when one recants them'. All this is very much in contrast with the impressions of the world that 'he' has just been recounting, which makes things and people seem so insubstantial that they could be swept away by the wind. Evidently by recounting them and forcing 'I' to accept his story, 'he' has recanted in some therapeutic way the sickness that troubles his soul.

The German word for 'recant' (*widerrufen*) has faint philological undertones of repeating something over again, rather as the English 're-cant' has. Kafka, as we shall see, makes much use of the double meaning of words, which comes about as a word passes to a higher, metaphorical level of significance. For he knows that it is in this way that the structure of thought is built up, partly providing a greater spiritual mastery over the world, but partly also producing a sense of increasing separation from it, accompanied by feelings of insecurity as language fails to fasten on anything real. The conversation that Kafka here holds with himself through the two voices of 'I' and 'he' is typical of all his future work which explores precisely this ambiguity in the nature of language. His writing might be described as an effort to set himself free from the insecurities and inauthenticities induced by his being an author. It is a kind of re-cantation of literature itself, that is, of the impression that words grasp reality.

## Hochzeitsvorbereitungen auf dem Lande ('Wedding Preparations in the Country', 1907)

'Wedding Preparations in the Country' is another story that exists in two versions, neither of which is complete – evidence again of Kafka's greater interest in the statement of a situation than in the development of a story. The story, such as it is, concerns the visit of an office worker to his fiancée in the country, an engagement about which he feels reluctant and guilty, and a journey that plunges deeper and deeper into rainfall and nightfall. Kafka is experimenting here too with those stylistic effects that are already beginning to be distinctively 'Kafkaesque', and such things as the progress of the plot or realistic characterization are almost irrelevant to this undertaking.

The conversation might be about Kafka's own attitude towards the conventional story-interest of fiction when Raban, the central figure, says: 'When one is about to embark on some enterprise it is precisely the books whose contents have nothing at all in common with the enterprise that are the most useful. For the reader . . . will be stimulated by the book to all kinds of thought concerning his enterprise. Since the contents of the

book are precisely something of entire indifference, the reader
is not at all impeded in those thoughts and he passes through
the midst of the book with them, as once the Jews passed
through the Red Sea.' This is how the reader of Kafka will pass
through his ever more inscrutable *œuvre* (inscrutable, that is,
from a realistic point of view), being stimulated to all manner
of thoughts about the enterprise of telling even the simplest
story, of telling in words what any experience is actually like.

In this connection, Raban makes one still more illuminating
observation, and one which throws further light on Kafka's
interest in the interacting points of view of 'I' and 'he'.

> So long as you say 'one' instead of 'I', there's nothing to
> it and you can easily tell the story, but as soon as you
> admit to yourself that it is you yourself, you feel as though
> transfixed and are horrified.
>
> (*Hochzeitsvorbereitungen auf dem Lande*, p. 8)

The remark reaches at once to the heart of existentialist understanding of the world. It is like a hollow, frightening echo of
Kierkegaard's more positive assertion that the individual is
higher than the universal. Language, however, is by nature
'universal'; it reduces what are essentially distinct and different
individual experiences to a standard set of shared words. Moreover, the standard set by language enables the individual to
judge the value of things, and above all what he himself is,
according to socially acceptable norms. He will understand his
place in the world so long as he uses its language with confidence, believing that what is generally said about people is
true also of his own experience. But he may develop the
capacity and desire to dissociate himself from the common
code; he may feel that he is acting a part when he performs
society's routine. And once he can self-consciously act the role
of living, able to see it and play it in his imagination, he is no
longer really bound by its conventions, but can look at it all
from the outside. He can see it all with a new vividness and
judge it by no conventional standard at all.

This position of being an outsider has been much idealized by minor exponents of existentialism, who have tended to confuse a nihilistic source of judgement with a positive one. Kafka certainly does not idealize it, as must be clear from the extraordinary simile he uses to describe Raban's imaginative position when he feels that he need not really go to the country in person to get married but will simply send his body:

> Can't I do it the way I always used to as a child in matters that were dangerous? I don't even need to go to the country myself, it isn't necessary. I'll send my clothed body. If it staggers out of the door of my room, the staggering will not indicate fear, but its nothingness . . . For I myself am meanwhile lying in my bed, smoothly covered over with the yellow-brown blanket . . . As I lie in bed I assume the shape of a big beetle, a stag beetle or a cockchafer, I think. (ibid., pp. 11 f)

It is an image we shall meet again in one of the best-known stories that Kafka ever wrote, 'Metamorphosis', where its significance will become even clearer.

Here we may conclude by stressing the extraordinary sharpness of visual perception that Kafka associates with this strange state of hallucinatory detachment from his body, and from the body of everyone and everything about him. It is because he sees their nothingness that he sees them so clearly. But just as it was difficult to define consistently the roles played by 'I' and 'he', so it is difficult to decide whether it is the external world that should be evaluated as 'nothing', or Raban's inner world. Kafka's technique in this early fragment is simply to juxtapose, and alternate, totally impersonal passages of objective detail with passages of totally subjective reflection. There is a disturbing lack of relevance or connection between them, and it is probably to this indefinable area, this metaphysical gap in the phenomenon of existence, that the word 'nothingness' most appropriately applies. Kafka's skill as a writer lies in his ability to make us aware of the presence of this nothingness. Whether the things on one side of this gap should be considered more real than the human consciousness on the other side is a question that cannot be answered; and for this reason reality and nightmare are ready to become confused, indistinguishable, and ultimately identical in Kafka's later work.

### Das Urteil ('The Judgement', 1912)

Neither of the fragmentary pieces discussed above is a love story, but both of them begin from a love situation, which then stimulates thoughts going far beyond itself. When Kafka wrote them he had, though not innocent of any amorous encounters, not yet met Felice Bauer. Their apparently harmless meeting took place on 13 August 1912; but a few days later Kafka recorded the occasion in his diary, concluding his sharp, un-flattering description of her appearance with the words: 'As I was sitting down I looked at her for the first time more care-fully, and when I was seated I had already an unshakeable judgement' ['*hatte ich schon ein unerschütterliches Urteil*'].

How fateful that look was, and how ambiguous that clear judgement! Was it a judgement on her or on himself? Earlier in the diary entry he remarks against himself how alienated he felt 'from everything good in its entirety'; and the first master-piece Kafka wrote, having the title 'The Judgement', deals with the fatal consequences – to himself – of a young man's an-nouncement of his engagement in a letter. Two days before Kafka composed this story during a single night of un-precedented inspiration, he had written for the first time to Felice Bauer.

Of this composition, which was to remain Kafka's favourite, partly because of the compelling power with which it had come to him, Kafka nevertheless used the painful image that was to haunt him five years later as a symbolic way of expressing the connection between his writing, his engagement, and his (in his view) self-inflicted tuberculosis: 'Then the wound broke open for the first time in one long night.' That not only this story, but also probably 'Metamorphosis' and above all *The Trial* are intimately connected with Kafka's relationship to Felice Bauer there can be no doubt. Unfortunately, this biographical information does not make the story, perhaps the most mysterious that Kafka ever wrote, any easier to understand.

The transition in this story from a description of commonplace events (a young man writing about his engagement to a friend living abroad), to an equally matter-of-fact account of very uncommon events (the son's being condemned to death by his father and going out to execute the sentence), is perfectly treated; the texture of the narrative, which is both normal and terrible, is quite seamless. The doddery old father of the first half who rises up at the end to pronounce judgement with the authority and effectiveness of a God-figure still remains at the same time a grotesque old man. His actions and remarks make no more and no less sense at the end than they do at the beginning, but they gradually acquire the power of life and death.

Why does Georg's father have this power over him? About six months after writing the story, Kafka felt prompted to 'write down all the relationships which have become clear to me as far as I now remember them' – he was then engaged in reading the proofs – and this particular question of the father's authority he answered as follows:

> . . . only because he [Georg] has lost everything except his awareness of the father [*Blick auf den Vater*] does the judgement, which closes off his father from him completely, have so strong an effect on him.
>
> (*Tagebücher*, 11 February 1913)

The diary entry as a whole stresses the obvious fact about the narrative that at the beginning Georg believes that he has a bond with his father through the figure of his friend, whereas at the end the bond seems to exist only between father and friend to the exclusion of Georg. If we ask again why this should change the father's position of initial weakness into one of such formidable strength, we find that what has really changed is the plausibility and effectiveness of Georg's position; it is his authority, his 'version' of his marriage, his friendship, and his filial devotion, which has collapsed. The reality of existence rears up in the shape of his father, rending the fabric of Georg's carefully considered thoughts (the letter writing doubtless symbolizes his belief that he has made sense of his life in words), brushing aside his last few strands of spoken protest, and destroys him.

The truly Kafkaesque quality of this story, in which Kafka for the first time fused the elements of his inspiration – hitherto expressed in fragmentary form – into a perfect whole, is easier to identify than to explain. It lies in the fact that Georg cannot see how monstrous and absurd his father's 'judgement' is. Or rather, he *can* see this, tries to defend himself with some facetious observations, but nevertheless obeys the judgement as though it were – in the words of his own diary entry – 'unshakeable'. What has collapsed is Georg's bond with commonsense normality; he is drawn by some inexplicable compulsion, which is as unhesitating as love and as irresistible as the urge to create, towards what he partly knows to be monstrous and absurd.

Doubtless it was in some such way that Kafka, who definitely identified his own fate with that of Georg Bendemann, remained neurotically obsessed with his father, his writing, and his fiancée. This similarity with the circumstances of Kafka's life has led critics to interpret the story in biographical terms. There are, however, some particular difficulties of detail involved in doing this; but before we look at these, there is one more general comment that must be made. The most disquieting question presented by 'The Judgement' is this: on what grounds does any judgement about what is monstrous and what is normal ultimately rest?

In the first instance, a man's judgements rest on convention, and at a deeper level they rest on faith. At the beginning of the story Georg gives a conventional account of his life to a friend. At the end, his faith in having the friend – that is to say, convention – on his side is shaken. Then psychological insecurities about the nature of his feelings for his parents and his bride drive him to commit suicide, while still mentally in alert possession of his faculties. Such subconscious compulsion, which reason is powerless to resist, is exactly what psychoanalysis regards as neurotic. In this connection two observations of Freud's are pertinent: first, that the private codes of behaviour and fantasy in neurotic patients often resemble actual moral codes, religious beliefs, and works of art, but are caricatures of them. Second, that where an obsessional neurosis is shared by a whole community it need no longer be regarded as sick and may very well be accepted as a religion.

In giving this account of the story, we have already come close to saying what the various characters 'stand for'. We did not quite interpret the friend as 'standing for' convention, however, but interpreted rather the psychological importance to Georg of having a friend, and hence of supposing (mistakenly) that he has a friendly relationship with his father through his friend. The psychological relationships within the story are clearer, in fact, than the characters of the persons between whom they exist; indeed, it is uncertainty about the latter that make the former so compelling. Much of Kafka's effect derives from the impossibility of interpreting – in the sense of 'referring to an external convention of meaning' – the three main personages.

On the simplest level of biographical interpretation, for instance, Kafka's actual father generally welcomed, rather than resisted, Kafka's marriage plans; and he did not claim (as the father in the story does) that his son's friends were really his own – these Herrmann Kafka did dislike. The friend represented in the story, moreover, does not appear to be an intel-

lectual of any kind, as Kafka's few friends actually were; the
most that we can be sure of is that he is a not very successful
business man, destined to 'irrevocable bachelorhood', and that
he is somehow not respectable in the eyes of Georg's fianceé. If
the father is a good family man (and has really been a businessman like Kafka's own father, even though not a very efficient
one in the son's eyes – another biographical detail that does not
'fit'), then his preference *for* the friend over his own son appears
to conflict with the fiançe's prejudice *against* Georg's having
such disreputable friends. Of course, one may interpret one's
way around these difficulties by saying that what the father
really wanted was an unmarried son, and that Kafka's 'letter to
his father' shows how deeply the son felt his father had made
it impossible for him to marry. Before venturing onto this un-
certain psychological ground, however, one simpler point has
to be made.

In the story Georg appears to be a very efficient businessman,
and he finds no problem from his point of view about marrying,
whatever difficulties there may be in getting his friend, his
fiancée, and his father to accept his plans. It is therefore
puzzling to see how Kafka can be identified with this character.
The only solution is to regard all the characters – including the
fiancée, for Felice Bauer (Kafka's fiancée) can scarcely be
supposed to have disapproved of Max Brod (Kafka's friend)! –
as relationships within Kafka's mind, as projections of different
aspects of his own psyche, and not as real people at all, or even
as symbols standing for anything outside himself.

Looked at like this, we can say that a *part* of Kafka was
conscientious and competent at the office, and did, as we have
seen, earnestly plan to marry. But in another part of his mind
Kafka had, as it were, emigrated abroad and had only a remote
and unsuccessful relationship to business; this part he knew
was doomed to 'irrevocable bachelorhood', and to imaginative
exposure to all kinds of danger. The crucial relationship with
the father also becomes intelligible once we regard the old man

not as an independent character, but again as part, the pro-
foundest part, of Kafka's psychological make-up.

A glance again at the 'letter to his father' will remind us how
little it portrays of an objective person (though it pinpoints a
few doubtless real characteristics) by comparison with the
subtlety of its portrayal of inner tensions within Kafka, who
pursues the ramifications of the relationship entirely within his
own mind, writing an imaginary answer from his father, then
answering that himself, and so on. Similarly, the father in 'The
Judgement' does not symbolize at all realistically a businessman,
or a family man, or any sort of bourgeois moral code or Jewish
belief (which Kafka's actual father did perhaps represent for
him). But this Kafkaesque father figure may symbolize
Kafka's private *relationship* to some or all of these things: his
relationship to the sources of his own life, to the inscrutable
and frightening fact of being alive, which he – like the rest of
us – tried to 'cover up' in conventional platitudes, pretending
it was normal when deep down he knew it was monstrous and
absurd.

The scene of 'covering up' is, as every critic has said, the
crucial turning point in the story. It is described as being done
with blankets because the German word for to 'cover up'
(*zudecken*) readily – and perhaps basically – suggests the idea
of a blanket (*Decke*); and as we have seen, it is by means of this
kind of linguistic association and concretization that Kafka's
creative mind works. But it is not a real man or literal father
that is covered up in any actual bed; it is the 'bed' or source of
Kafka's creativity which a part of himself tried to smother with
conventionality, at this moment in his career when he had become established in his job and considered marrying. The part
that was in danger of being smothered, the creative part, in
other words, which Kafka knew to be deeply associated with
*his* relationship to his father – although Herrmann Kafka, the
man, was in reality hardly a very inspiring figure – then rose up
and 'killed' Kafka. The 'wound', as he described the experience

of writing this story, was mortal. He was now a true writer; and a writer, as Kafka wrote to Max Brod, 'dies (or doesn't really live) and is perpetually sorry for himself'.

## Die Verwandlung ('Metamorphosis', 1912)

'Metamorphosis' was written only a month or two after 'The Judgement', in the same period of intense inspiration that produced also substantial parts of a novel – later called *America* – to which Kafka gave at the time the significant title, 'The Man who Died Away' (*Der Verschollene* – another example of a word that has come to be used metaphorically in everyday speech, to mean 'missing' or 'forgotten', but which is in fact the past participle of the verb *verschallen*, to 'die away' of sound; sounds and silence, noises and listening, had all kinds of symbolic overtones for Kafka's imagination, as we shall see later). This story is again about a man who dies, 'or doesn't really live', and it is conceived in such a way as to extract the maximum of humour and pathos from this piteous fate.[1] It indeed expresses the writer's desire to be 'sorry for himself', but certainly in no romantic or idealized way; the device of having the hero wake up to find himself transformed into a beetle renders the whole situation absurd.

Alas, all too many critics have treated 'Metamorphosis' with humourless solemnity, defending the beetle's point of view as though it provided a serious criticism of bourgeois society with its narrow-minded conventions and false values. The story seems to me to provide nothing of the kind. If it carries any criticism at all, then it is directed as much against the beetle as against anyone else. And to the extent to which Kafka identified himself with Gregor Samsa – he saw similarities between the hero's name here, as with Georg Bendemann's in 'A Judgement', and his own; and we have noted already that the early hero, Raban, also felt like a beetle, besides having a name that can be associated with Kafka's own (a 'raven' resembles a 'jackdaw', which is what *kavka* means in Czech) – the criticism is directed once more against himself. It is, however, less a moral criticism, let alone a social one, than a psychological critique, or analysis, of what writing does to the world and to the self. It 'transforms' both of them beyond recognition, as the title of this story (in German) already implies.

Laboriously to point out each of Kafka's humorous–pathetic effects would be to ruin them every one. Suffice it to say that they result from everybody's efforts, including the beetle's, to do something appropriate to the situation. Since there is no known cure for having turned into a beetle, nothing is appropriate and every response is absurd. This is not to say that every response is the same: the chief clerk's pompous speeches are clearly different from the mother's sentimental sighs and shrieks, the father's self-assertive hostility from the sister's selfless sympathy. But they are all engulfed in the same absurdity, and while this gives them a momentary 'depth', they quickly sink to the bottom where nothing matters any more.

It is remarkable how Kafka manages to sustain our interest for as long as he does, giving to the story an illusion of suspense and movement, as Gregor and his family show signs of coming to terms with what has happened, and even hope that something else will. The reader almost forgets what it is that has happened and that it is absurd to expect anything could be done about it to make it bearable. Is Gregor beginning to feel a little better as he learns to beetle about the walls and ceiling, does his sister care about him more or less, will the family survive . . . ? But what on earth are we talking about – the family has a beetle in the house instead of a son! There can only be one solution to this absurd problem and all the equally absurd personal reactions and domestic crises to which it gives rise; and that is death.

Astonishingly, Kafka even contrives to give to this foregone conclusion a hint of further, even positive meaning. It is as though Gregor's final disillusion, suffering, and death had become a kind of self-sacrifice, almost an act of expiation, which has redeemed the whole family in some way. It is no more than a hint, and it too trembles on the brink of nonsense; for the way this family has been 'saved', if that is what the ending means, is by first turning one of its members into a beetle and afterwards getting rid of it.

But naturally we know better nowadays than to deal with a work of literature, and especially a modern work, in so simple-minded a spirit. We have learnt to recognize symbolism when we see it. And the symbolism of this story is plain: here is modern man in his alienated condition, treated as an insect by his fellows who think only of appearances, frustrated in his inner longings which he is unable to communicate, swept away good-humouredly but forcefully by the unsqueamish prole-tariat, and all the while an unacknowledged religious victim . . . or words to that effect.

Now, it is worth reminding ourselves that we do not have to accept the effect of words as true just because they have been used 'symbolically'. Symbolism has become for students of literature a magic concept to conjure with: find the symbolism in a poem or story, its 'deeper' meaning, and its value is estab-lished (and the value of literary criticism). But if literary criti-cism is not to degenerate into a lesson in sophistry, teaching in effect that anything can mean anything, we have to judge for ourselves not just whether there is symbolism in a work but whether we accept that symbolism as true, whether the symbol has been well chosen, i.e. on what grounds and for what pur-poses.

There is nothing particularly mysterious about the way Kafka achieves his effects in 'Metamorphosis': he simply con-tinues to describe Gregor's thoughts and feelings as though they were human, while everything connected with his bodily condition, such as his physical ability to see and speak is reduced to the level of an insect. The device could hardly be more artificial; it is certainly no less so than the allegorical make-believe and puppet shows of medieval literature. The difference in Kafka's case comes about from his having used a realistic style of presentation; but this should not deter us from asking what the purpose of his patently absurd invention is. Simply to jump to the conclusion that it shows symbolically how absurd conventional living is, would be to remain entirely uncritical in the face of a particular kind of literary effect.

What, then, is the literary effect produced by Kafka's grotesque invention? Strange to say, the predominant one is rather familiar, rather old-fashioned, and not at all symbolic: it is what in English we might call 'Dickensian' – and Kafka was much impressed by Dickens – and are inclined to regard as an amalgam of sentimentality, humour, and pathos. The swooning mother, the bemedalled father, the sweet-natured sister playing the violin: this is the stuff of which a certain kind of Victorian novel is made. Indeed, a large number of novelists throughout Europe in the nineteenth century were drawn towards the subject of poverty, lower-class family life, and the psychological problems of a social code based on money and respectability, even if they did not all go to the harrowing lengths of describing the womenfolk ruining their eyesight over badly paid sewing and lodgers lording it over a humiliated household, as Kafka does here.

Quite apart from these emotionally obvious themes, there is the detailed description of quite commonplace events that is common to all novels written in the style known loosely as 'realism' – as though opening a door or crossing a room or the words people actually use in daily speech or the clothes they actually wear were more 'real' than anything recorded by writers about life before Kafka writes sentences crammed with observation and suspense to describe Gregor's efforts to open a door. It is a breathless, climactic passage: will he manage it? What will happen next? Now, if we ask why this scene is so gripping, we see at once that it is solely because 'he' is a beetle. And the pathos, humour, and sentiment of all the scenes mentioned above are due of course to the same cause. The symbolism of this story, that is to say, the literary device upon which it is based is undoubtedly important and illuminating. But what it illumines is not so much any real defectiveness in society as one source of realistic effectiveness in literature.

In reopening the question of what Kafka's symbolism means, we are in danger of starting too soon on a much larger problem of interpretation, before we have looked at enough examples of his writing. The larger issues will be left till the last chapter, therefore, and the immediate question of what 'beetledom' meant to Kafka pursued further here. The words Kafka uses to describe Gregor's state (*Ungeziefer*, *Insekt*, *Käfer*) doubtless had connotations and associations for him that are less evident in English: a dirty little monster, a creature divided into sections, a being imprisoned – the word *Käfig*, a cage, has alliterative similarity to *Käfer*, and it was through hints of other meanings hidden in words, which in this case again resembled his own name, that Kafka transformed the world.

He was also interested in the ambiguity of a closed-in state: did it imply a stronghold and security, or imprisonment and deprivation? A notebook entry reads simply: 'My prison cell: my fortress.' The postures in which Kafka later describes his 'hero' elaborate these associations. Gregor is now imprisoned in his room which gets into a more and more filthy state; he is divided in two, in that he has the mind of a man and the body of a beast. The most revealing features of Kafka's symbolism, which are at the same time entirely 'naturalistic', come from the beetle-man's ability to lie on the ceiling, a position where he feels 'more free', and from the concession he gains from his family after he has been *wounded* (an idea associated with writing for Kafka, as we have seen), to watch their everyday life through a chink in the slightly open door. Nothing could symbolize more exactly the position of the writer as an outsider looking on, a situation in which many of Kafka's contemporaries found themselves and also found their inspiration:

Proust and Mann (whose *Tonio Kröger* Kafka admired),
Joyce, and Yeats, who also declared, 'I must lie down . . . in
the foul rag-and-bone shop of the heart.' It is to the conditions
under which 'he' has been 'allowed to find the Archimedean
point' of effective literary portrayal that Kafka's beetle symbolism points above all.

Kafka forces us to ask a question that has only recently
started to receive much critical attention: from what *point of
view* does a novelist write, on what attitude to life is fiction
based ? The question is of acute importance because the amount
of 'social' criticism contained in many realistic novels seems to
be high, and has come to be accepted as useful for purposes of
education and even of sociological research.

The implication of 'Metamorphosis', then, is that the
novelist's viewpoint is unnatural and even disgusting. The one
fatal thing to do (for someone in Gregor's 'position') is to let
oneself be carried away by the deceptive lure of art, by its sweet
suggestion of an emotionally and imaginatively more satisfying
world. Gregor's death results from the scene where he leaves his
prison in response to his sister's performance on the violin. He
wants to bring her back to him, who truly appreciates her, to be
with him in his foul beetle-room, to really live with her again.
He forgets what he is – which is to say, he forgets what the condition of art is. The outrage he feels at the philistine human
beings who are listening to her as well, but do not (he senses)
appreciate her, together with his desire to save and possess the
promise of beauty he hears in her music and remembers in his
heart, are vitiated, of course, by his monstrous appearance as a
beetle. If we interpret the symbolism of *this* situation, we see
that Kafka is casting the gravest doubt upon the emotional
responses of the artist, and upon his indignation at society. He
is saying 'in effect' (that is, by showing from what point of view
such literary effects are achieved) that the pathos and satire of
the realistic novel are the products of a degraded and deluded
vision – a beetle's vision.

Kafka reveals, by his grotesque reproduction of Dickensian effects, to what extent the sentiment they evoke differs both from that of moral satire and from that of tragedy. There is nothing besides sentiment in the protest of realistic fiction of this type: beneath the surface of humorous–pathetic satire there is a *totally* hopeless situation – beetledom. The effect of realism is to make us feel that something ought to be done to improve men's misfortunes in society – and so it should! – but Kafka betrays the literary secret of this way of writing. It makes something appear to be society's fault, and so capable of improvement, that is in fact past all remedy: beetledom. And here we have to ask whether we believe Kafka's symbol to be generally valid (and it is a matter of religious faith), for what it implies is that man is as hopelessly and inappropriately situated in the world as a beetle would be in a human family. And that the most he can hope to achieve is an impression of that family's being better off – redeemed – in some way when it has got rid of an unwanted spiritual perversion in its midst. We have to decide how trustworthy we find a beetle's point of view to be.

## In der Strafkolonie ('In the Penal Settlement', October 1914)

Kafka lived through the period of the First World War, which was to put an end to the Austro-Hungarian Empire and to make the social order of most European countries look like an *ancien régime* that could never return; but even in his diaries and letters he rarely mentions this cataclysm, the world's first experience of modern war, which was soon to alarm the imaginations and conscience of so many – although at one time Kafka considered volunteering for military service, from which he was officially excused on grounds of poor health.

'In the Penal Settlement' is a story, however, that might be interpreted as an exception to Kafka's customary reticence on the subject of the war and of the public world generally. It is certainly a story that concerns bloodshed and discipline, and the conflict between an old-fashioned military code and new attitudes of liberal humanitarianism. The fact that it is not about trench warfare, or indeed about warfare at all, need not discourage interpreters of a later generation, who have grown used to hearing war described in terms not of heroism and duty – the rhetoric still heard publicly in Kafka's day – but of a 'machine', a war-machine, which is the metaphor that forms the basis of this gruesome story. The metaphor is presented literally, of course, in the imaginative manner with which we should now be becoming familiar in Kafka. 'In the Penal Settlement' is about an actual machine, a horrible invention of Kafka's, that puts men to death in accordance with ancient law and custom.

The old law, for which we see a prisoner about to die, is very simple; it is based on obedience to the law which itself turns out to be supported by illegible or otherwise incomprehensible writings; for the prisoner is illiterate and the narrator, who is represented as a detached, scientific observer, can also make nothing of them. The officer who champions the old order claims that the machine is so designed that the condemned man will, as the machine slowly tortures him to death, 'get the point' of the law whose meaning or verdict has never been explained to him in words. This metaphor – though it happens not to be available in German (others are) – has, as it were, been taken literally in Kafka's story: the meaning of the deadly punishment is slowly cut deeper and deeper into the body of the victim by the sharp points of the machine.

The judgement to be thus physically 'borne in upon' the man on this occasion is: 'Honour thy superiors!' (*Ehre deinen Vorgesetzten!*) which carries in German perhaps a clearer suggestion that an old order of things, and not just a chain of command, has to be maintained. Now, as the story continues, we see how this order is already being undermined, cannot be maintained, and eventually goes to pieces. Again, these metaphors are illustrated literally: the machine has not been kept in good working order, and eventually the mechanism goes wrong and murders in a quite unforeseen fashion the officer who has always believed in it. The reasons why the upkeep has been neglected might very well be seen as an allusion to actual political developments in Europe generally before 1914. In Germany and Austria, for instance, the approval of the military budget had for years been a major political issue; so had the whole question of the role of parliament and the spread of democratic ideas; and in England the cause of women's votes was also involved. These are the factors also at work in the 'penal settlement' that have quite changed the way in which ritual executions are carried out. There was a time when each execution was a public occasion, almost a festival, watched and applauded by women and children. Even the victims were ecstatic in their agony, to judge anyway from the expression the officer recalls seeing on their faces as they got the point of the time-honoured code.

There are many such details having a possible relevance to the 1914 war, which revealed its murderous character already in its opening months (on the Marne, at Tannenberg, on the Galician front). Even the grisly humour of the story, which depends on the same kind of contrast exploited in 'Metamorphosis' between attitudes of sensible, human concern and a basically inhuman situation, might be said to apply to the way the army 'takes good care' of the very men it will sacrifice as cannon fodder. But there are also, of course, several important features of the story that do not seem to have any connection with the war, or if they are meant to have one, represent it falsely. For instance, the officer class in no sense sacrificed itself *instead of* its men, even if it (in some cases) entered the fray to prove the justice of its cause. Perhaps it was possible to believe in 1914 that 'the war to end all wars' would release the common people and put an end to the military caste; Kafka had certainly read revolutionary writers like Bakunin, Herzen,

Kropotkin, and attended occasional meetings of the anti-militarist 'Klub mladých' and the working-class 'Vilem Körber'. But why is the Old Commandant, who actually invented the dreadful machine, buried in the local tea-house, having been refused burial by the church? After all, military men in the past were generally given splendid funerals by church and state alike; why *this* suggestion of disgrace here? By telling us that 'the priest wouldn't let him lie in the churchyard' and showing us the grave in a tea-house 'that made . . . the impression of a historic tradition of some kind', Kafka inevitably starts off in our minds thoughts of a quite different interpretation. This interpretation is strengthened as soon as we glance again at Kafka's biography.

July 1914 had been a fateful month in Kafka's life for quite personal reasons. The shots fired in Sarajevo were unimportant beside the sentence he felt had been passed on himself in the Berlin hotel where, before witnesses, his engagement to Felice Bauer was formally dissolved. Kafka likened the occasion to a court of law (*ein Gericht*) at which he kept silent. This silence is stressed as a feature of the story, where it distinguishes the last moments of the machine as it goes wrong and murders the officer: scarcely a very appropriate detail to characterize any aspect of the First World War, but rather more relevant to Kafka's experience of writing – at night, in solitude, and silent. And the detail which makes least sense as regards the war and the military, namely, that the officer subjects himself to punishment by the machine, makes most sense when interpreted in autobiographical terms: this was exactly how Kafka described his extraordinary viewpoint as a writer 'that he had turned it against himself'.

The result of Kafka's turning of his intelligence on himself, instead of upon life, was to put an end to the long-drawn-out torture of a love story that was no longer capable of producing the ecstatic sighs of tradition – another puzzling detail if the story is supposed to be about war – and to abruptly kill the man

in charge. Who, then, is this man, and what is the machine he
operates; and why does the machine go murderously wrong
under the gaze of the rationally detached onlooker – and who
anyway is he? A biographical interpretation leads naturally to
the answer that all represent parts of Kafka's personality. The
machine, in particular, looks very much like a pictorial representation of the self-torturing process of writing as Kafka
experienced it. The part with the points is called by Kafka in
German *der Zeichner*, and it writes the words of the 'judgement' into the flesh of the condemned man (*der Verurteilte*) –
expressions which recall Kafka's conception of artistic activity.
And not only Kafka's. His contemporary, James Joyce, with
whom he has more similarities than has generally been recognized, describes in *Finnegan's Wake* how Shem the Penman
writes world history as he cowers in his pitchblack house
O'Shame, using his own skin as paper and his own bodily fluids
as ink:

> . . . with this double dye, brought to blood heat, gallic acid
> on iron ore, through the bowels of his misery, flashly,
> faithly, nastily, appropriately . . . [this] first till last
> alshemist wrote over every square inch of the only fools-
> cap available, his own body, till by its corrosive sublima-
> tion one continuous present tense integument slowly
> unfolded all . . . cycle-wheeling history (thereby, he said,
> reflecting from his own individual person life unlivable,
> transaccidented through the slow fires of consciousness
> into a dividual chaos, perilous, potent, common to allflesh,
> human only, mortal) . . .

Kafka likewise, beginning from his 'own individual person'
and finding 'life unlivable', condemned to a slow death of
shame for some unknown guilt, transformed this experience
'through the slow fires of consciousness' into a story that is not
the 'dividual chaos' of Joyce's *œuvre* but is in some way related
to a turning point in world history.

If we assume that 'In the Penal Settlement' is not so much *about* any single, identifiable reality, in the sense that realistic literature usually appears to be about some one thing, but is a symbolic 'world' in its own right, then it is possible to refer it *both* to Kafka's biography and to the First World War. The onlooker, whose visit to the settlement provokes the crisis of the story, has only one word to say: 'No.' He rejects the traditions on which the cruel machinery – of writing and of war – has been justified. When the disciple of these traditions turns the machine against himself, it not only kills him but 'no sign was visible of the promised redemption; what the others had found in the machine the officer had not found'. Some part of Kafka, then, did not believe either in war or in writing.

This part was what we have called Kafka's essentially modern, sceptical intelligence. And the strength of his negative belief, his 'no', his inverted theology (as we have called it) was such that it could establish a bond between private and public experience, between poetry and war: a negative bond. The cruelty of existence is, after all, merely intensified by war, not created by war. Men suffer in any event more or less; and all must die. The crucial question for a writer is not whether he has got his historical facts right, whether his realism is true; the reality of suffering and death is known to him through his imagination, and the question he must decide is what it means – i.e. his symbolism must be true. Literature has since the earliest times offered symbolic statements of life's cruelties, which in art appear irradiated by beauty, a convention that has been publicly accepted as meaning that human suffering is redeemed when the point of life's law is borne in on us in this way. But to the sceptical onlooker of 'In the Penal Settlement', whose gaze is fixed upon the sun, as though upon the bright light of a higher truth, all the beautiful writings of the past, like the skilled workmanship that went into designing the now dilapidated machine, have become unintelligible and unacceptable.

Finally, then, we can say who the Old Commandant 'is' and

why he is buried in the tea-house. He designed the machine, which is a perfect expression of the skills of the old order. He is the man who was once so idealized in European culture, the artist who beautified life's pain, and who (in this story) did so not only in exquisite – even if now incomprehensible – writings and designs, but executed them in life besides; or more accurately, executed other people by this means, thus persuading everyone to see that justice was done and life redeemed. He could symbolize, therefore, that ideal man of the Renaissance, skilled equally in art and in living, a 'complete' man like Leonardo da Vinci, or more recently, Goethe. It was a type, and an ideal, much discussed by Kafka's intellectual contemporaries, often in the terms made fashionable by Nietzsche who called this secular redeemer 'the superman'.

Such a type would necessarily be refused burial by the church, not only because he stands for this-worldly redemption, but because he had, as Nietzsche recognized in his feud with Wagner (whom he once thought possessed such superior greatness), great similarities with the actor. The church used to refuse burial to actors, because men who spent their life play-acting could not be trusted to have authentic souls. Their place of rest, in Kafka's imagination if not in any real instance, is appropriately enough a tea-house, a *café*, such as had been the non-home of all rootless intellectual life in Europe since the mid-nineteenth century. That is where the spiritual idealism of Europe's cultural tradition had been buried, driven out by more modern trends of a democratic, liberal kind – trends that Nietzsche despised with an aristocratic disdain typical of many writers of Kafka's generation, though probably not of Kafka himself.

Kafka sensed rather some danger that the old order might be revived. There is a vague sense of menace about the inscription on the Old Commandant's grave, set up by 'his adherents, who must now be nameless . . . There is a prophecy that after a certain number of years the Commandant will rise again and lead his adherents from this house to recover the settlement.' Let critics beware, who have been struck by phrases like 'rise again', 'redemption', and even mingling of 'blood and water' in this story, and not jump to the simple-minded conclusion that Kafka is prophesying the return of Christ. Doubtless the old order he has described was religious in origin, but he has discredited it thoroughly. The kind of reactionary revivals that were likely to issue from the intellectual atmosphere of the *Kaffeehäuser* of central Europe, let alone from the sleezy *Bierkeller* which this tea-house rather resembles, were not in the least Christian, though they certainly had a bogus religious–aesthetic appeal.

### Der Bau ('The Burrow', 1923/4)

'The Burrow' is one of the two last stories that Kafka wrote – the other, *Josefine, die Sängerin*, will be discussed in the last chapter – and its symbolism points unmistakably towards his own life and work, and (by comparison with 'In the Penal Settlement') to very little else besides. It is about an animal which works with its head and hands to construct a subterranean dwelling. This is what in English is naturally called a 'burrow', but the German word suggests a more concrete edifice. The ambiguity brought out by the difficulty in translating the title is illuminating and helps to explain a puzzling passage at the core of the story.

For a burrow is essentially a hole made in solid ground; at the same time that it is a construction it consists of nothing at all. It is thus an altogether fitting final symbol for the kind of writing Kafka had striven to produce from the start: something that would be of real importance to him and yet also nothing at all. Burrowing is a metaphor for thinking and writing, which creates an insubstantial inward realm, a spiritual labyrinth beneath and within the hard ground of existence. Here the self who is the narrator, has tried to make himself secure, both from the predatory animals that live and hunt for food above ground, and also from a dread beast, an unknown enemy that likewise burrows from within, and one that the self knows in the end he cannot evade.

Kafka's narrator says of his burrow: 'I built it for myself and not for visitors,' a declaration that reminds us again of his desire to have the bulk of his writing destroyed, and makes us hesitant to pry into these transparent symbols. For what can the last enemy be in this story but the tuberculosis that had for so long been undermining Kafka's health and was by this date about to bring about his death? And what can the 'small fry' represent if not the minor ailments that also lurk within any body, but cause no concern because they do so little damage to the system. The pathos and interest of this story depend, as they do in 'Metamorphosis', on the hopelessness of trying to do anything about the basic situation. The burrower tries this device and that, pins his hopes on some truly impregnable work, experiments with leaving the burrow for ordinary life above ground, but is drawn back and left desperately regretting that he had not worked on a different plan from the beginning.

Kafka's metaphor enables him to describe the most subtle perceptions of existential psychology in the most lucid images. For instance, the burrower recalls 'happy periods in which I could almost assure myself that the enmity of the world towards one had ceased . . . or that the strength of my burrow had raised me above the destructive struggle of former times'. He finds, however, that it is impossible to rest upon 'the strength' of any spiritual achievement, although he admits that the desire to do so is 'a fancy [which] used to have such a hold over me that sometimes I have been seized by the childish wish never to return to the burrow again, but to settle down somewhere close to the entrance, to pass my life watching it, and gloat perpetually upon the reflection – and in that find my happiness – how steadfast a protection my burrow would be if I were inside it'. In other words, the mind longs to possess its own achievements, the self (of a writer at least, so Kafka explained in the letter to Max Brod already quoted above, p. 20) cherishes the childish fancy of wanting to get outside itself and enjoy itself from without.

Kafka is describing an impulse that Kierkegaard and Sartre have defined in much more elaborate language of despair and bad faith – terms that are necessarily negative because the self-conscious mind can only recognize its *inability* to achieve identity with spontaneous being. Kafka visualizes the same desperate situation in terms that have the positive vitality of a story, and thus do, in a sense, achieve a positive triumph over the very negativity of the spirit's position that they characterize.

The most remarkable instance of Kafka's imaginative transcendence of his own dilemma comes in the central passage where he gives an account of his plan for the castle keep (*Burgplatz**). The name of this central stronghold of his burrow recalls his largest, but incomplete draft for a novel, *The Castle*, and Kafka makes us feel here what the writing of this novel meant to him and what he wanted to achieve with it:

> One of these favourite plans of mine was to isolate the Castle Keep from its surroundings, that is to say, to restrict the thickness of the walls to about my own height, and leave a free space, and not without reason, as the loveliest imaginable haunt. What a joy to be pressed against the rounded outer wall, to pull oneself up, let oneself slide down again, miss one's footing and find oneself on firm earth, and play all those games literally upon the Castle Keep and not inside it; to avoid the Castle Keep, to rest one's eyes from it whenever one wanted, to postpone the joy of seeing it until later and yet not have to do without it, but literally hold it safe between one's claws,

* An English reader is likely to imagine a solid, heavily fortified tower when he reads of a 'Castle Keep'. The German word, however, suggests primarily an open space albeit within castle walls. (The 'castle' is, of course, a closed, 'locked' place, in either case, even though Kafka here uses the word *Burg* rather than *Schloß*.

a thing that is impossible if you have only an ordinary open entrance to it; but above all to be able to stand guard over it, and in that way to be so completely compensated for renouncing the actual sight of it that, if one had to choose between staying all one's life in the Castle Keep or in the free space outside it, one would choose the latter, content to wander up and down there all one's days and keep guard over the Castle Keep.

(In *Beschreibung eines Kampfes*, p. 202)

The description is, of course, very similar to the one quoted earlier describing the burrower's desire to possess his burrow from outside. The paradox of this desire is better brought out here for the simple reason that the plan to build this moat of freedom around the Castle Keep is more clearly an absurdity: it is a hole built around a hole, and at one point in the description Kafka plays nicely on the German word for 'foundation' and 'reason' (*Grund*) that would be good enough to support such an extraordinary project. Once we try to focus our imagination on the kind of wall that could separate one hole from another, so that he could 'play all those games literally on the Castle Keep and not inside it . . . [and] literally hold it safe between one's claws', we realize that Kafka is giving a precise symbol for the mysterious, insubstantial nature of language: resting on who knows what real foundation. Source of some mysterious source of comfort, creating the illusion that one can hold some essential meaning safe between one's claws, and inspiring in Kafka particularly the desire to play 'games' on the literal meanings of words within whose metaphorical realms we normally dwell on trust. Kafka was ready to leave what is for most of us the closed 'castle-square' of the mind, inside which language imprisons us, in the hope of embracing it in freedom and unassailable security from outside.

The more closely we look at this and other stories by Kafka the more we discover, of course, that he is for ever narrating, in a basically static, symbolic manner, the same situation. All his narratives are in a sense disguises and delays, a 'postponing of the joy of seeing and yet not having to do without'. And as he says, this is a 'thing that is impossible if you have only an ordinary open entrance', that is, if the reader is allowed to penetrate openly into the stronghold of Kafka's language. That is why we are told, in the opening sentences of the story, that: 'all that can be seen from the outside is a big hole; that, however, really leads nowhere; if you take a few steps you strike against natural firm rock'. This hole is the remains of an 'abortive building attempt' – an attempt on Kafka's part to write openly about himself, as he often appears to do; but as he shows, his writing is impenetrable in 'natural' or openly biographical terms.

At a considerable distance, yet still 'in the vicinity', there lies the real entrance, covered only by 'a movable layer of moss' where he is completely vulnerable. He is vulnerable because he wants to be able to 'leave at a moment's notice if necessary', i.e. because he cannot commit himself totally to his inner world, nor yet live a life above ground either. Kafka was not, in fact, an aesthete in the sense of a writer who believed he could bury himself totally in the ivory cave of his art. His strength, and superiority to many modernists, lie in his profound feeling for the reality of life against which the negative phenomenon of consciousness and all its works contrasted for him so strongly. Indeed, the vivid value of his writing, so full of dreadful tension despite being so apparently empty of real content, was inspired by Kafka's readiness to keep alive this sense of contrast, moving to and fro between the realms of art and life like the creature in 'The Burrow'. What he achieved was a uniquely heightened sense of awareness – an awareness not so much of anything concrete in the external world as of a very real state of danger in man's spiritual condition. 'Is not full awareness the true definition of a state of danger?'

# 3

# The Novels

That Kafka's genius may have been better suited to the short story form is an idea that we took up briefly at the beginning of the last chapter. We may add here that memorable parts of the novels could be considered as short stories in their own right, and several of them were actually published on their own (whereas the novels only appeared after Kafka's death and none of them is complete). Thus, the first chapter of *America* was published in three separate editions of Kurt Wolff's series *Der jüngste Tag* (1913, 1916, 1917/18) under the title *Der Heizer* (*The Stoker*). Admittedly, it is there called 'A Fragment', but in a letter to Wolff, Kafka suggested that this piece would make an ideal book if published together with – not the rest of the novel, as we might expect! – the stories, 'Metamorphosis' and 'The Judgement', for they 'belong together both inwardly and outwardly, there is an obvious and, even more, a hidden connection between them . . . The unity of these three stories together is just as important to me as the unity of any one of them.'

A similar situation exists with regard to that part of *The Trial* which Kurt Wolff published as an individual story in 1915 and again in 1917 under the title *Vor dem Gesetz* ('Before the Law'). And at least one part of *The Castle*, the main sections of Chapter XV, has all the makings of a Kafka story; the very fact that these sections have individual titles 'Amalia's Secret', 'Amalia's Punishment', and so on – could indicate perhaps that Kafka himself was thinking of possible publication separately from the novel. Nevertheless, it is on his incomplete novels that

Kafka's international reputation now rests, despite their unfinished state and the uncertainty about whether Kafka wanted them to be published at all, and we must now turn to *The Trial* and *The Castle* and consider to what extent they represent genuine extensions of Kafka's accomplishment. Lack of space forbids discussion of *America* (*Der Verschollene*); this is a pity in that it achieves some striking 'surrealistic' effects – German critics have likened them to those of the contemporary school of expressionist writing and even painting in Germany – but they are not typical of Kafka's future development and the novel is considerably inferior to the other two.

## Der Prozeß (The Trial, 1914)

Kafka's fame began to grow fast with the interest aroused above all by *The Trial* in France soon after the Second World War. It was discussed by writers of the stature of Sartre and Camus, dramatized for a successful stage production, and clearly spoke to the imagination of a considerable French public. The reason is obvious, of course: here was a story, by a Jewish author, of unjust, insane persecution, with a hero who resists the tyranny of arbitrary and inscrutable authorities, even though he cannot hope to break their total power of life and death. The relevance of this symbolism to recent history in Europe seemed so profound that it was hailed as prophetic, while the similarities between Kafka's manner of thinking and existentialist philosophy, which had likewise acquired a reputation for political commitment to the cause of freedom, also helped to establish him as a forerunner and an ally. Whatever the merits of French existentialism as a political philosophy (which have been cast in doubt by Sartre's later development), the political relevance of Kafka's novels, and particularly of *The Trial*, has gradually come to be seen as rather more questionable.

*The argument against treating* The Trial *as political satire*

The details of the novel do not, in fact, throw much light, not even satirical light, upon the way in which political and social persecution actually occurs. The most inappropriate feature of the story from a realistic point of view is the way the hero is left so largely free in public life, able outwardly at least to go about his ordinary business. When he is 'arrested' he is free to telephone a lawyer if he wishes, and later in the novel he discovers he can engage as many lawyers as he likes. He is even asked whether *he* has any objections to the proceedings against him being conducted on Sundays or during the night; and these all-powerful authorities that 'persecute' him inhabit old attic quarters to which they seem almost ashamed to summon their victim. These are *not* characteristics typical of any secret police yet known to the world; nor is it very common for any members of any persecuting organization to suffer corporal punishment when one of their victims complains about the way they have treated him.

The chapter entitled 'The Beater' (*Der Prügler*) is crucial in this context, because the justification given by the beater of his activities – 'I'm employed to beat people, so I beat them' – has been seized on again much more recently (for instance, at the time of the Eichmann trial) as epitomizing the inhumane mentality inculcated by a modern bureaucracy, where people do their jobs, no matter how cruel these may be, simply because they are employed to do so. The machine they serve relieves them of any personal sense of responsibility. Now, as a psychological insight into the way actual employees behave in the world, Kafka's remark is not particularly original; it does not differ greatly from Shakespeare's observation regarding the callousness of a gravedigger (in *Hamlet*), to the effect that: 'Custom hath made it in him a property of easiness.' What is original and disturbing in Kafka's beating scene are the weird circumstances in which it takes place – in the hero's own office, in an old store-room he had never been in, and apparently being repeated every time he opens the door – and the no less strange behaviour of the hero himself.

Although he makes some attempt to stop the beating from being carried out, he does so by resorting to private remonstration, even bribery, although he is in a public building where help could easily be found. But K. does not want help, he slams the door shut upon the disgraceful scene, because he evidently feels implicated himself in its disgrace. It is, in fact, K.'s disgrace, and he feels it to be his private responsibility in a way that makes it impossible for him to call for help from other people. There is, however, one thing he can ask the office clerks to do: 'Clear that lumber-room out, will you? We're being smothered in dirt!' K. obviously does not expect the clerks to find any actual people in this little room, let alone any beating going on. The place has another symbolic dimension for K., which it does not have for them; its symbolic suggestiveness causes this scene to occur in K.'s consciousness.

Let us accept, then, that *The Trial* cannot be read as even a symbolic account of totalitarian persecution, simply because the whole of the uncanny train of events narrated here are responded to by the hero in a manner that makes no political sense. Kafka creates the impression that K. is himself provoking and even controlling these events, from the fateful moment when he presses the bell in his bedroom at the beginning – police agents do not wait for a citizen to press the bell to call them in – until the moment near the end when he is told: 'The court receives you when *you* come and it dismisses you when *you* go.' (My italics.) It might be possible to persist with a political interpretation to the point where it is held that the victims of persecution themselves provoke their fate, but there is no historical evidence to support this view. (This argument sounds a little like the mad logic of tyrants who are ready to see everything a citizen freely does as suspicious and 'evidence' of a guilty state; it is an argument that cannot be used to interpret

Kafka's novels, however, since these are written from the stand-
point of the victim, not of the persecutor.)

## The biographical background

What other kind of interpretation can be offered of this novel,
once its relevance in detail to the historical circumstances that
brought it fame is ruled out? Who or what is it that has
'arrested' Joseph K., the doomed hero of our time? We have
met this question before, in fact, in our discussion of Kafka's
stories. Why does the doomed creature of *Der Bau* go back to
his burrow? He says already well before the end, 'Someone
whose invitation I shall not be able to withstand will, so to
speak, summon me to him.' Why does Georg Bendemann in
*Das Urteil* execute his father's mad sentence of death? The only
explanation of his guilt that is given is that: 'You were really an
innocent child, but still more really you were a devilish human
being.' What is this more than real reality in which Kafka's
heroes are 'sinful irrespective of guilt'?

It is tempting to return to the facts of Kafka's life for a fuller
explanation of the mystery. This novel is all about a 'trial',
albeit in a most unusual court of law; but the 'court of law'
(*Gerichtshof*), as Kafka called it, was also most unusual when
sentence was passed on him – as he felt – in the Berlin hotel, the
Askanischer Hof, on the occasion of his breaking off his engagement to Felice Bauer. We know also that this novel was
written in the months following that break and would appear,
with its obsessive theme of some private guilt, to have been
largely inspired by it. A modern critic, accustomed to the
dependence of a work of art on the psychology of the artist
rather than on the reality of the world, will inevitably start to
notice such 'revealing' details as that the initials of Felice Bauer
are the same as those of the girl who, at the start, means a lot to
Joseph K. in his trial, Fräulein Bürstner; or that a minor but
attractive part is played in the novel by a girl called Erna, which
was the actual name of Felice's sister; and so on. Yet this kind

of information does not help us very much, for the obvious reason already given, that Kafka has made such a strange use of whatever autobiographical material he may have incorporated in the novel, and it is precisely the significance of this strange use that we should be endeavouring to understand.

## Kafka's use of language

The problem the novel raises for us is indeed connected with the significance of names, persons, and even events in Kafka's life; but the problem is a linguistic, rather than a biographical or even psychological one. What do the words mean with which Kafka has represented what happened in his life, thereby distorting it so strangely? This is a problem of truly general, and essentially philosophical interest, for it makes us wonder at the process by which language makes experience comprehensible to ourselves and communicable to others. How well do the words we use actually 'fit' the reality of what happens in the world? This is a question to which we must have an answer – or else a sense of trust that conventional language does mean something – and yet we ultimately cannot answer it. Kafka is writing in this novel, and to some extent in all his work, about this problem: about what words 'really' mean, about their conventional meaning often smooth with well-worn metaphorical usage, and about the dark, inscrutable background that lies behind this reassuring facade.

When Joseph K. discovers the scene of a beating in the office store-room, he not only slams the door on it, he goes over to a window and gazes out. He has had a glimpse of some deeper reality and now he tries to penetrate its meaning – 'to pierce the darkness of the courtyard', or more explicitly in German: 'mit den Blicken in das Dunkel eines Hofwinkels einzudringen'. Let us not labour the symbolism of what 'court' (*Hof*) this now is, but simply ask what K. is trying to do in this moment of penetrating contemplation, when we might have expected some more conventional action from him. He is making 'a vow not to hush up the incident', a phrase that does not reveal to an English reader what Kafka's commonplace German expression plainly states: 'Er gelobte sich, die Sache noch zur Sprache zu bringen' – to put the thing, or case, or cause, into words. It is a matter of language.

Inasmuch as this is what the novel explores, namely, the linguistic, and not the legal or moral, essence of K's. case (*Sache*), a great deal of its significance gets lost in translation. Even the title of the book is misleading, for although the English 'trial' has more than one meaning, the connotations of the word are different from those of the German one. *Der Prozeß* is cognate, of course, with the English 'process', and Kafka uses the term interchangeably with *das Verfahren*, which means 'procedure', but also has undertones of 'entanglement' and even 'muddle'. Joseph K.'s trial is thus a verbal process, the process whereby we try to investigate with language what the matter with our lives is, getting hopelessly entangled 'in the process'.

It is, as James Joyce knew, quite simple to construct an 'action' out of plays on words, but it is probably impossible to produce the same pattern of verbal 'cases' with English words as with Kafka's original German one. For instance, it is just as easy for an English as for a German reader to see that the initials for Fräulein Bürstner are the same as Felice Bauer's, but no amount of ingenuity can communicate the sexual echoes of *bürsten*, a word that Kafka would surely have known as a vulgar expression for intercourse. Similarly, the mysterious 'authorities' who try Joseph K. symbolize verbally the spiritual predicament a man finds himself in as soon as he asks questions about language. For the German *Behörde* has a philological groundwork, a foundation in a more 'real' reality, which is of the greatest interest. Cognate with it is the word for 'to belong' (*gehören*), which in turn goes back to the basic word for 'to hear' (*hören*), and to words describing ancient conditions of servitude (*Hörer, Hörigkeit*); *gehörig*, on the other hand, is a common modern word for 'appropriate' or 'relevant', with legal overtones of competence and admissibility.

The authorities before whom K. stands, therefore, are a symbol for some of the most fundamental questions raised by man's capacity to reflect about his position as a thinking, word-using animal in the world. To whom does he belong, who hears him, what words are appropriate to his situation, whom should he obey and who is competent to judge him? The consistent way in which Kafka's language creates an appearance of concrete action and character out of his basically spiritual, abstractly philosophical preoccupation with the 'world' of consciousness, becomes still more apparent when we look at other words closely connected with the above. K., for instance, is subjected to cross-examination, which in German is *Verhör*, with undertones of hearing incorrectly. Yet another train of words is based on the process of exploration downwards (*untersuchen*), as well as on concepts of what is right, embodied in persons K. only hears about but never meets (*Untersuchungsrichter*).

### Interpretation of the action and the characters

Once we assume that this is in part what *The Trial* is 'about', we can go on to interpret various aspects of the 'action' and of the 'characters' accordingly. For example, Joseph K. has to decide whether to get a lawyer to represent him, and then when he grows dissatisfied with this character's ability properly to represent his case, whether and how to get rid of him. Who is this character and why is he presented as a sickly, bedridden old man, who would be of no interest to K. at all if he did not have a sexy girl in his house to look after him? The answer is that he represents a character called in (ad-vocatus) to represent K.'s case; this he is too feeble to do, however, because K. is instinctively interested less in tiresome discussions of meaning than in its dependence on sex, which seems to have some intimate relationship with it. The lawyer thus 'represents' a character in a new sense: he represents Kafka's feeble reliance on characters (other than his hero's – and not even on his in any naturalistic sense) to further the 'action' of his unique kind of spiritual inquiry. Kafka uses the word *Vertreter* (representative) interchangeably with *Advokat* (lawyer), and we learn that there is a 'difference between a lawyer for ordinary legal rights and a lawyer for cases like these . . . The one lawyer leads his client by a fine thread until the verdict is reached, but the other lifts his client on his shoulders from the beginning and carries him bodily without once letting him down until the verdict is reached, and even beyond it.'

There are many clues in this chapter to show the reader that this passage, and the characters and situation described in it, represent different kinds of literary, rather than legal, practice. One of them lies in the word *Eingabe* (petition), which it is the representing lawyer's task to handle; a very similar German word from the same root means 'inspiration' (*Eingebung*). K.'s attitude towards his representative is unconventional, by comparison with that of an ordinary client like Kaufmann Block. The word *Kauf-mann* (business or tradesman) is given overtones of venality, because Block has apparently bought the services of many representatives; he is like a hack novelist, always looking for a new way to put his case. And the kinds of representative that he chooses are doubtless the ordinary ones referred to above, who lead him on through a rather tenuous tale. Kaufmann Block is simply a rather poor writer – his 'petitions (inspirations) turned out to be quite worthless' – who turned to matters like these only late in life, after his wife had died. He has no business to invoke the help of an *advocatus* like K.'s, who has specialized in the much more difficult kind of 'practice, in which after a certain moment nothing essentially new ever occurs'.

K.'s *Advokat*, however, is surely one of those lawyers who wants to 'lift his client on his shoulders and carry him bodily, without letting him down, until the verdict is reached and even beyond it' (. . . trägt ihn, ohne ihn abzusetzen, zum Urteil und noch darüber hinaus). This is a description of Kafka's 'practice', or at least of the one he has been looking for from the beginning, and it recalls details from the stories, from the early 'Description of a Fight' in which his first characters rode one upon the other's back, to the inescapable verdict of 'The Judgement', where there was no longer any possibility of being 'put down' again on to the ground of common-sense reality; a world in which metaphor, the process itself of language, becomes a nightmare-reality in its own right.

In ordinary literary terms the verdict to which a writer is exposed is merely the verdict of the public on his work. He does not 'do' anything criminal, but simply goes on with the process of writing, and this 'process' – as the priest explains to K. near the end – 'gradually passes over into a judgement' (geht allmählich ins Urteil über). In Kafka's case, we know that this verdict, which essentially he passed on himself, however he might represent it in writing (as being, for instance, the 'judgement' of his father), had the force of a 'life-sentence' – a play on words that is not possible in German but comes near to the spirit and goal of Kafka's work, just as it does to that of James Joyce whose *Finnegans Wake* is also a kind of never-ending 'life-sentence'.

It is significant that Joseph K., like his author, declares that he is not interested in knowing 'the meaning of the sign' that causes his public, at his first interrogation, to applaud or to hiss. He is aiming (like his author) at something more serious than ordinary literary success. He has a spiritual cause to champion: the cause, the case, of all individuals who have been 'arrested' like himself. For here everybody and 'everything belongs to the Court', even though most of the people he meets seem quite unconcerned at the fact, even unaware of it. (Kafka evidently thinks like Kierkegaard that all men are in despair and anguish at their human condition no matter whether or not they realize it.) But the fact that all men are subject to the process of living,

which most of them do not think about enough to realize that
it is (metaphorically) a nightmare, does not make the plight of
the individual less grievous. The more desperately he pursues
his case, the more inevitable the verdict becomes.

Thus, K. cannot make common cause with other men:
'combined action against the Court is impossible', which is to
say that mankind cannot achieve through the solidarity of some
public convention or belief any release from each man's private
'trial'. Nor can he dissociate himself from other men entirely.
As with the animal in 'The Burrow', who can neither stay up
above in the world or down below on his own, so Joseph K.'s
case is inextricably bound up with his having a public existence
which he keeps up right to the end: 'had he stood alone in the
world, there would have been no case'. In other words, he
realizes the nature of his own individuality through contact
with other people. They have a part to play in the process
through which the fateful verdict is reached. It is through this
relationship to the others that the self realizes what it is.

It is not solely through a relationship to another person that
we come to realize the unique character of the self as a state of
consciousness; we may discover it more immediately through
our relationship to our body. This is how Joseph K. first discovers it. For the figures who break in on him one morning,
eat his breakfast and steal his clothes, are certainly not secret-
policemen but rather representatives of his own body. They
beg K. to stop protesting about his position and asking for
their 'warrant' for being there. Why on earth, they exclaim,
'can't you accept your position and why are you so intent on
pointlessly annoying us, who are probably closer to you than
any of your fellow human beings!' The symbolism could
scarcely be more obvious, and it is supported by many
associated details, that call attention to the base, bodily
character of these men, 'bodyguards' (*Leibwächter*) of the
spirit, who later have to be ascetically punished and chastised
for taking liberties to which they are not entitled. The liberty

that K. desires is a pure, spiritual freedom, a total *Freisprechung* (absolution) through words. It was, of course, Kafka's own desire as a writer, an aspiration to emerge victorious over the monstrous 'process' (trial?) of being a thinking, speaking person in a world where language does not ever seem to 'apply'.

This novel is about the futility of man's 'applications' (*Bittschriften* – indeed, the novel is itself a *Bittschrift*), and about the very serious consequences to his body of repeatedly making them. We know how ruinous to Kafka's health writing was, and how he associated literature with illness; K.'s health similarly suffers as the 'process' continues – and in the last scene he is put to death 'like a dog'. These famous final words suggest that it is a bodily fate, which he cannot control, that at last overtakes him, even while his mind is battling to argue still and hope. The last thing he sees are his strange executioners observing the *Entscheidung*, an almost untranslatable word in this context, for it means the outcome of the story, but also suggests a decision or judgement of some kind, and has undertones of division and separation. The separation is between K.'s mind and body; the decision is his own; the outcome inevitable. The logic of this situation is 'unshakeable' (*unerschütterlich* – the word Kafka used to describe his sense of 'judgement' on looking again at Felice Bauer), but 'it cannot withstand a man who wants to go on living'. Alas, the novel has made it quite clear that K. did not simply want to go on living; he wanted to know. The outcome, decision, separation was for Kafka inevitably fatal.

The style of the final chapter – to the extent to which it is finished – is particularly grotesque. Two more men are sent to execute K., who are less realistic, more absurd characters than the warders who came to arrest him in chapter one. They look to K. like 'tenth-rate old actors', then again like tenors. Outside in the street they grapple hold of him in such a way that the three become a unity – 'a unity such as almost only lifeless matter can form' ('wie sie fast nur Lebloses bilden kann'). The trio move wherever K. wants to go; he catches sight of Fräulein

Bürstner, or a girl resembling her, and like a single man they follow her: 'that he might not forget the warning that she signified for him'. The lesson is plainly stated: 'he suddenly realized the futility of resistance. There would be nothing heroic in it were he to resist . . . to snatch the last appearance of life by struggling.' So K. does not resist, but co-operates, even getting himself and his executioners past a policeman who might have intervened. Only at the last he cannot seize the knife, 'as it was his duty to do . . . and plunge it into his own breast . . . He could not relieve the authorities of all the work, the responsibility for this final mistake lay with him who had denied him the last bit of strength necessary for the deed.'

While a biographical interpretation could explain this scene perhaps by reference to the grotesque 'performance' in the Berlin hotel, when Kafka's fateful separation from F.B. was conducted largely by others, the question still remains why Kafka has presented it like this at the end of *The Trial*. From a literary point of view, the scene is a travesty, a deliberately non-heroic ending. The executioners who are even more closely linked with K.'s person than the warders, symbolize his rapidly ailing state. When K. was first 'arrested' (*ver-haftet*), his spirit was brought to a halt in mid-career; both the German and the English word suggest this coming to a standstill and being held fast. Throughout Kafka's writing there is a constant play on images (often very common words) of movement and standstill; their conflict is as fundamental as that between freedom and imprisonment, or silence and noise. What is ambiguous is which is the better state. This last chapter describes a series of sporadic movements as K. half runs to meet his fate, half tries to stop it still. But since, after a year of futile 'trial', he no longer knows what he wants to stop it for (certainly not for F.B.), he can only acquiesce as his body performs the inevitable last act. In just this way Kafka was to describe his outbreak of tuberculosis three years later: as his lungs taking on the burden of suffering which his spirit could no longer bear.

## The material and the spiritual

In making this kind of interpretation, we are beginning to distinguish between what 'is' (or stands for) body and what is spirit in Kafka, between reality and consciousness, in a way that his manner of writing renders finally impossible. Thus, the ubiquitous organization that has arrested K., with its endless hierarchies of officials, can be looked at symbolically as meaning either or both of two totally different things. One interpretation might see these authorities as symbolizing the infinite ramifications of consciousness, with airless corridors of thought, and impenetrable realms of speculative inquiry. Why else should people wear cushions on their heads, if not to symbolize the pressure upwards of the mind, always eager to break out of any constriction?

Many other details concerning the Courts suggest, however, that they are anything but a symbol of man's spiritual state. Their law-books are obscene, their practices corrupt, especially in their claims on women. The reactions of the women themselves, both in this novel and in *The Castle*, are equally ambiguous. They seem to have intimate connections with the courts, even belonging to them in some ill-defined sense; at the same time they fall in love with men who are accused and 'arrested', i.e. men who are in conflict with the Courts. Finally, the attitude towards women of the hero in each novel confirms this ambiguity. K. finds Fräulein Bürstner and Leni – later it will be Frieda and Pepi – attractive because he has been arrested and the women seem (at first) to offer something that he deeply needs. This something could be the solace and promise that have always been associated with love; but Kafka's love scenes give a more sordid impression of mindless sex.

Now, again, we have to be clear about what is original in Kafka's representation of ambiguity in the nature of love, and more broadly in the nature of reality. It is not the ambiguity itself, but Kafka's way of representing it, that disturbs us.

Indeed, by making it appear to be totally a problem of representation, he makes it appear quite hopeless, irrational, and fatal. That is to say: we do not need to look very far in literature to discover that love has another side that is hostile to the spirit – 'the expense of spirit in a waste of shame'. Nor (to be more precise) that a writer will be particularly sensitive to the question: 'What boots it with uncessant care / To tend the homely slighted Shepherd's trade, / And strictly meditate the thankless Muse? / Were it not better done as others use, / To sport with Amaryllis in the shade, / Or with the tangles of Naera's hair?' But the problem that confronts K. no longer appears in this light, and it is Kafka who has changed the lighting.

The biographical experience from which he started, of uncertainty and even incapacity concerning marriage, is not in itself so extraordinary – to the extent to which we can talk of an experience 'in itself' apart from a man's reaction to it – as Kafka well knew from reading of similar experiences in the lives of Grillparzer, Kierkegaard, and Flaubert. Kafka places this experience in a new and unrecognizable light, and in so doing puts it beyond man's moral control or even rational comprehension. All forms of moral or rational presentation assume that we can recognize what is right and wrong, better and worse, in the world; even if we make the wrong choice, we can know when we do. And this in turn assumes that the character and meaning of reality does not depend entirely on our interpretation of it; that the world is distinct from human consciousness, which can thus hope to penetrate and master its laws. Kafka's writing totally undermines these assumptions. We are no longer sure what is 'there' in reality, and what exists in K.'s mind. Does he confront a symbol of the natural world, physical existence in its sordid, obscene inscrutability? Or a symbol of his own consciousness, a projection outwards of his own muddled nature, which takes on a semblance of evil reality? Kafka's literary achievement consists in his having made it possible to distinguish between these two things. His symbolism is, as we have said, total, and leaves nothing outside itself to which it can confidently be referred, or on which a distinction between reality and consciousness can be based.

## The meaninglessness of meaning

The impenetrability of the world's law is summed up most brilliantly in this novel in the separate story already referred to: 'Before the Law', which is preached by a priest to K. as a parable. He has already been warned by the artist, Titorelli, that the court before which he is being 'tried' is 'completely impenetrable by argument' or more exactly: 'Impenetrable by arguments that one brings before the court . . . It is quite a different matter with one's efforts behind the public court, that is to say in the consulting rooms, in the corridors, or for instance in this very studio.' The word 'impenetrable' is in the German *unzugänglich*, which the first translator (Edwin Muir) rendered as 'impervious'. Whatever undertones an English reader may find in these words, it is important to notice how much more readily concrete the German *Zugang* is; it can mean an entrance or gateway, as well as 'access' in a more metaphorical sense. In Kafka's parable this situation is visualized concretely: a man waits before the entrance to the law all his life, and never gains admittance. The situation seems hopeless partly because the man insists on waiting for access. But when, after the parable has been told, K. himself tries to argue his way into the meaning of the story, he is unable to base any conclusive arguments on it, i.e. to reach any conclusion in either a negative or a positive sense.

K. cannot even prove, for instance, that the man who waits away his life has been deceived; that would at least establish a rational criterion of truth external to the story. However, at the same time that no truth can be established literally, so that in this representative symbol (if it is one) the mind's situation before the law of existence is hopeless, the story itself captures this very situation perfectly – and that, as the artist says, 'is quite a different matter'. This parable is preached to K. for a *good* reason: it is his story. Literally speaking, in terms of the novel as a whole, this parable does not do K. any good; it does not help him to evade his fate, does not procure for him the total 'acquittal' (*Freisprechung*) he seeks.

What, after all, would total release from the 'charge' of living mean? 'The documents relating to the case are said to be completely done away with, they vanish entirely from the proceedings, not only the charge, but the trial and even the acquittal itself is destroyed, everything is destroyed.' It sounds like Kafka's wish that his own manuscripts should be destroyed! But even while he knew that literally his writing could not save him, Kafka could imagine perfectly the hopelessness of desiring that it should. This parable represents a moment when the mind totally grasps its own situation, a moment of pure freedom such as the animal dreams of in 'The Burrow', an impossible and 'untenable' position like the Archimedean point only to be reached on condition that it is turned against its possessor. At this point in the book, the meaninglessness of the whole 'trial', the process not only of writing – as we have provisionally interpreted *der Prozeß* here – but of existing consciously at all, is concretely symbolized. The novel grasps itself in a symbol that passes beyond any interpretable meaning, for it symbolizes the impossibility of interpretation. 'The text is unalterable and the opinions [of critics] are often only an expression of despair at this fact.'

## Das Schloß (The Castle, 1922)

*The Castle* is Kafka's *magnum opus*; though it is flawed, unfinished, and perhaps unfinishable (whatever Kafka may have told Max Brod about his plans for a conclusion), it establishes its own imaginative world on a scale and with a unity of atmosphere that are unmatched by the earlier novels. Even *The*

*Trial* moves between two worlds still, one of them that of an ordinary office worker, the other a Kafkaesque realm of spiritual experiences that have become more real than everyday reality. When K. enters the frozen village of the Castle, he has left behind for ever the world of normality, though he can remember one and occasionally refers to it (did he have a wife, a job, a home there? Could he leave the Castle precincts again and emigrate to some normal country with a name?). The completeness with which Kafka's hero has severed his connections with the ordinary world is reflected in his loss of any name: the hero of *America* is called Karl Roßmann, the hero of *The Trial*, Joseph K., the hero of *The Castle*, simply K.

The action of the novel is likewise less attached to recognizable situations in 'life' – as the cathedral scene is in *The Trial*, for instance, where Joseph K. is sent by his real-life boss to accompany a visitor to the firm on a sightseeing tour of the town. The reality in which the Castle is located resembles far more that of the parable preached in the later course of the cathedral chapter. The whole of this novel is a projection of the concept of impenetrability (*Unzugänglichkeit*), of waiting 'before the Law'. And a large amount of the novel is taken up with interpretative discussion, similar to that which followed the narration of the parable in *The Trial*. The difference in *The Castle* is that the problem of interpretation is not discussed in a reality distinct from that of the stories K. hears, nor does such discussion take place in a reality distinct from the one in which K. works (as is the case with *The Trial*). There is only one reality in *The Castle*; the stories K. hears are about events that have actually taken place there, and his discussion of their meaning implicates him in their outcome.

## K.'s struggle for freedom

This is not to say that the kind of interpretation we have made of *The Trial* cannot be applied to *The Castle*. On the contrary, it must simply be taken further. *The Castle* is just as much about the mind's efforts to grasp its own activity; and it is as deeply embedded in the paradoxical limitations of language and thought, which can 'know' that something lies beyond themselves but cannot reach it, and which cannot procure the services of any other instruments – 'employees' or 'servants' are Kafka's typically concrete symbols here – more dependable than themselves, more 'in the know', in order to attain this end. All that can be ascertained for sure is that in trying to attain it, in trying to 'get above himself' spiritually, in order to pin down the answer to his own existence, he fails, and achieves nothing but humiliation, guilt, and finally – to judge from the way the novel is going – a kind of defeat by self-attrition.

Kafka is less concerned in this novel with the guilt aspect of this problem, although some critics have interpreted the book realistically as showing K.'s treatment of Frieda to be morally wrong (and even referred the story to the quite real relationship of Kafka to Milena Jesenská, which may have inspired some of it, though these facts bear little resemblance in detail to those in *The Castle*). More important here than his desire to prove his innocence is K.'s fight to get the upper hand and be free – though, as we have already seen, the word used in *The Trial* for 'acquittal' (*Freisprechung*) suggests the idea of getting free from entanglement in the muddled proceedings (*Verfahren*). Guilt is incidental and hardly provides a plausible explanation of why K. fails. His failure lies in the nature of the 'case', or in the nature of 'the Castle' (*Schloß*), the locked, inaccessible place, to use the metaphor on which this novel is based. All the hero can accomplish is to clarify the fact that everything he knows about the castle is confused, contradictory, and senseless. By putting up a steady rational struggle against its confusions and contradictions he does achieve a kind of freedom – but it is a negative freedom, such as that described at the end of chapter eight:

> . . . as though he were now indeed (*freilich*) more free than ever, and at liberty to wait here as long as he desired, in

this place usually forbidden to him, and as though he had won for himself this freedom such as hardly anyone else had ever succeeded in doing . . .; but – this conviction was at least as strong – as though at the same time there was nothing more senseless, nothing more desperate, than this freedom, this waiting, this inviolability.

(*Das Schloß*, p. 145)

## *Kafka's use of language in* The Castle

Unlike many modern philosophers – Wittgenstein, it should be remembered, was Kafka's near-contemporary in time and cultural milieu – Kafka knew that a mind that has disentangled itself from the confusions of language, and detached itself from the closed rules of mental 'structures' and language 'games', is in a state not of positive freedom but of despair.

The use Kafka makes of the double meanings and deeper associations of words has been more widely and clearly recognized with regard to *The Castle* than with regard to the rest of his work. Apart from the title, and the suggestive name of Frieda, whom K. woos as a 'Freier' (again implying one who frees), K.'s questionable role as a Land Surveyor (*Landvermesser*) has undertones of foolhardy boldness – 'getting above himself' ? – as well as of measuring inaccurately. *Klamm* is not only an adjective meaning tight and hemmed in, but has associations with the word for 'brackets' (*Klammer*), an important concept at the time in the phenomenological philosophy of Husserl, who was similarly exploring the possibility of 'bracketing' reality, in the sense of grasping its meaning immediately, without reference to outside, metaphysical postulates of understanding and evaluation.

A thought which particularly interested Kafka was the mind's dependence upon the way in which it first receives, or conceives, an idea; so much else seems to follow inescapably from the context in which a word or image arouses our attention. Kafka expresses this thought concretely, of course, as an actual situation of arrival in a place from which traditional preoccupations of the world have (as Husserl might have said) been 'bracketed off'. Here Kafka's hero 'is received in a way that perhaps had determined the direction of everything that followed' ('daß der Empfang vielleicht allem Folgenden die Richtung gegeben hatte'; *Empfang*, it should be noted, is a word that associates the two ideas of reception and conception). Kafka says the same thing in the context of another story – 'A Country Doctor' (1916/17) – when he writes: 'Once answer a false ring at your night-bell and you can never repair the damage.' To some imponderable degree K.'s fate depends upon the fact that a character called Schwarzer 'happened to have' a girl-friend at the inn where the story of K.'s struggle with the Castle begins.

We should not, however, wax too ponderous over this problem, however much it may exercise K. himself along with the other accumulating details that he tries to make sense of. For we can see, as K. cannot, that we are reading a book in which the author is inventing these details. If we ask to what purpose he invents them, we can only answer: in order to symbolize the inscrutability of the mind's inventions. 'Inventions' are things which 'come in' from outside. Like K., they find themselves at the Bridge Inn, a place of transition, where a first thought begins to develop into something else. Like the *Bittschriften* in *The Trial* which represent what the novel also is, so this opening scene of *The Castle* represents symbolically the process of opening a novel – or of beginning on any train of thought. The hero can thus wonder whether he is playing the right role: should he perhaps have come as something other than a Land Surveyor – after all, it seems that no land surveyor is needed, there is no job for him to do – and is his engagement in this role, as he says, 'only a pretext, they were playing with me'?

## Similarity to earlier works

There are many features besides these in *The Castle* that recall Kafka's earlier work and reinforce the interpretation we are making here. K. stands alone, confronting a 'singular' reality, not a plural one, as he thinks at first. There is no difference between the world of the castle and the world of the village; everything belongs to the castle, as it did to the courts of *The Trial*. The apparently tri-partite division of the world, which Kafka first symbolized in 'The Judgement' and then analysed in his 'Letter' to his father, turns out to be a bi-partite one at best: for the other two parts beside himself are united against him, being in league despite all appearances to the contrary. They may quarrel, abuse, seduce one another, and generally present to K.'s mind a picture of universal injustice. But these others scarcely seem to mind. K. is amazed that a castle official like Erlanger summons people in the middle of the night, keeps them waiting on his whim, and that nobody objects, though their discontent is general. Of the whole relationship between castle and village he is told: 'In your opinion it's unjust and monstrous, but you're the only one in the village of that opinion.'

K. plays again the solitary role here that the narrating voice plays throughout so much of Kafka's work: that of the upright, rational, self-willed individual who demands his rights, and especially his freedom, in the face of an absurdly distorted and corrupt world, wherein he can find *no one like himself*: no one who can represent his case, no one – in the language of *The Castle* – who can act as a messenger, a contact, with the reality beyond his own mind. Kafka's ability to symbolize this state of mind, divided from the public world to the point of schizophrenia, refusing to compromise with anything that the world finds normal, protesting therefore about everything because the protesting gesture of refusal is the only one he knows, has made him the foremost myth-maker of the twentieth century. The myth does not describe very well the social facts of totalitarian persecution, as was at first supposed. But it does symbolize most profoundly the spirit of a hopelessly protesting generation, a generation of individualists without a public cause.

*The insoluble paradox*

So, we find here again that K. wants everything to be done on his initiative and on his own terms. 'I don't want any act of favour from the Castle,' he declares, 'but my rights.' The reader cannot help wondering, as with the man who passed a lifetime waiting 'before the Law', why K. does not simply go away. The question is even raised in the novel, and K.'s answer is (equally simply) that he has come in order to stay. There are characteristic shades of Jewish humour in a reply that says only that he would not have taken all this trouble to come, if he could be satisfied with merely going away again – shades that darken into profounder thoughts about what the difference is ultimately between a question and an answer: life *is* like that, and where should we go away to out of life?

K. is struggling for 'official' permission to stay – and there is much play with words like *hierzubleiben, standzuhalten, festzustehen*. But this is a permission that is not given to the kind of bold, inquiring, self-conscious mind that K. typifies; once a man no longer takes it for granted that he has a place 'here', he will never obtain any explanation of what his place is – except on his deathbed perhaps, when it will have to be recognized that he has in a sense possessed it all along. Why, then, the reader may wonder (as various critics have done) does not K. simply settle down in the village? Are there not hopeful signs that he is learning to do so towards the end, where he seems to acknowledge his mistake?

> I'm not sure if it's like this, and my guilt isn't clear to me either, but when I compare myself with you [Pepi] I do seem to get the idea that perhaps we've both been trying too hard, too noisily, too childishly, too ingenuously . . the way a child clutches a tablecloth but gets nothing besides knocking down the whole treat, which it has then made unobtainable for itself forever.
>
> (*Das Schloß*, p. 407)

Close reading further reveals that in the last chapter of *The*

*Trial* K. likewise recognizes how he has always wanted 'to reach out into the world with twenty hands' (mit zwanzig Händen in die Welt hineinfahren) and that 'this was wrong'. But close reading should also reveal that K. co-operates with his executioners in the end; that he sees the futility of resistance (*Widerstand*); and that he finally admits to them: 'I really didn't want to stop' (*stehenbleiben*). And plain common sense should tell us that a mind like K.'s cannot possibly 'settle down' in this crude and primitive village with its low-browed, sullen peasants, rank bathhouses, and orgiastic pubs. Even if, as seems most probable, the village is not meant to be believed in as any real place, but accepted rather as a symbol of Kafka's inner world – where icy conditions of intellect coexist with the physical crudities of bodily existence – it is still impossible for a Kafka-esque intelligence to find its earthly condition anything but utterly strange and unacceptable.

## The fantasy of fulfilment

The only times that K. ever feels himself at one with anything are when his conscious mind is lost. For instance, he enjoys in his first encounter with Frieda 'hours in which they breathed as one, hours in which their hearts beat as one'; but at the same time K. knows that he is 'losing himself or wandering into a strange country, farther than any man had been before'. He enters this strange country (*Fremde*) again much later in the novel when he falls asleep on Bürgel's bed. The scene has some similarity with the one in *The Trial* where K., at a moment of critical interest to himself, just when his uncle and his lawyer are discussing his case, goes off to 'sleep' with Leni. In the *Castle* scene, K. merely goes off to sleep (by himself) just as Bürgel is about to explain to K. how he might gain access to the castle. If this were a realistic novel, we should feel disappointed that the hero had missed this opportunity to gain his goal; we might even feel that some moral criticism was implied, and that we had been shown some tragic flaw in human nature. But since the novel is not of this conventional type, such criticism would make no sense. We have no confidence that anything really worth having could come from this, more than from any other, encounter with a character employed by the castle; Bürgel is as implausible, bedridden, and tedious as the rest. We can ultimately not even be sure whether K. has missed or got what he wants when he goes off to sleep. For his sleep 'was not a real sleep, he heard Bürgel's words better perhaps than before when he had been awake but dead tired, word for word beat upon his ear, but his burdensome consciousness had vanished, he felt himself free, it was not Bürgel who held him any longer, only he groped occasionally out for Bürgel, he was not yet in the depth of sleep, but he had gone beneath the surface'.

If K.'s experience here is to be related to anything in the real world, then it must surely be to Kafka's experience of writing late into the night, trying to gain access to the castle of his mind, encountering fictitious personages and situations that are in every sense mere diversions, and finally being no longer 'held' by one, so that his conscious attention wavers, sinks beneath the surface of consciousness, gropes for this murmuring figure once or twice more, then plunges into pure fantasy. K.'s fantasy is one of triumphant conquest, a struggle with some now archetypal artistic figure who cannot resist K.'s 'advances'. In this semi-conscious realm 'beneath the surface' the components of K.'s (or Kafka's) psychic world are laid bare as in a depth analysis. K. wins applause, a public toast in champagne – a banally obvious symbol of success. The figure whom he conquers 'looks very like a statue of a Greek god' – the classic model of accomplishment in Western art. At the same time this figure is a 'secretary', a castle employee, that is to say, Kafka's symbol for a servant of the literary imagination; the very word has philological undertones of secrecy – *secretarius*, a confidential official. And this secretary now vainly tries to cover his 'secret parts', giggling like a girl. Is *this* what K. wants, then? Is his desire a sexual one? Up to this point, K.'s dream might have been invented by Freud, but here Kafka's intelligence goes beyond that of his great contemporary. K.'s fantasy takes him further: the girlish, secretarial god disappears, so too does the applauding public, and K. discovers he is alone, eager to pursue the struggle but unable to find his adversary. To find him again, K. must wake up (woken by a pricking sensation – he dreams it is a *broken* champagne glass: i.e. his subconscious rouses him with a sense of failure). And once he is awake again, trying to focus his conscious mind upon its impossible task – impossible because the focus *is* so concentrated – K. 'understands completely' that there is nothing else he can do except go completely to sleep: to sleep and not to dream, and thus 'go away from everything' (*allem entgehen*).

K. is now 'dead to the world' ('abgeschlossen gegen alles, was geschah'). Bürgel meanwhile goes on talking, and what he describes is something very like K.'s own situation viewed from the outside. K. is no longer the hero, but is in Bürgel's words about to turn into the client who 'has never yet been seen, but always expected, expected with true thirst, and always regarded as unobtainable, which is only logical'. Bürgel has longed for just such a client as this, whose 'silent presence is an invitation to penetrate into his poor life, to transmute oneself into him as though into a possession of one's own and to suffer with him in this pretended guise'. If Bürgel could achieve this he would have 'ceased to be an official employee' (*Amtsperson*), he would be 'unable to refuse any petition' (*Bitte*), he would be 'in despair, or looked at more accurately very happy'.

What is the meaning of this imagined situation, so strikingly resembling K.'s own, which is preached over his uncomprehending head, like the sermon in *The Trial*? Why does Bürgel say that here, 'in this very situation, the client in all his helplessness . . . can master everything, and need do nothing to achieve it except produce his petition', only to conclude, as K. wakes up and hurries to another official who hammers on the wall, that: 'Thus the world corrects itself in its course and keeps its balance . . . There are opportunities indeed which are simply too great to be made use of, there are things that are destroyed by nothing but themselves'? As in the sermon story, the language has a prophetic or oracular ring, Greek this time rather than Hebraic, as though some ultimate mystery of human existence were being formulated, some ultimate limit of human endeavour, beyond which nothing mortal may go, however much imagination may desire it. And so it is. The limit here symbolized is that which prevents just this: prevents a man from becoming a creature of his own imagination, and wakefully in all conscience enjoying the fulfilment of his dreams. It is a state of despair and happiness to be able to imagine what it would be like to be another person, to find another character for oneself. Kafka here imagines the still more complicated possibility of what character he (as K.) might assume in another character's eyes. But however many reflections upon himself a man makes, he is not the same as any of these images. Fully to enter into the opportunities offered by any imagined reflection, the real man would have to be 'dead to the world'. A man cannot consciously possess himself, i.e. be identical with his longed-for fantasy-image of himself.

*Semantic ambiguities*
While Kafka's ability to symbolize this impossibility, this limit of consciousness, does not depend on any unique characteristics in the German language, he is very sensitive, of course, to those aspects of German that reflect his preoccupations. Thus, he remarks, for instance, on the fact that the word for 'his' in German is the same as the verb meaning 'to be' (*sein* *). Kafka picks up this detail because it could be said to typify the kinds of ambiguity and confusion to which all language gives rise, inviting us to build structures of thought, and hence apparent

* The point is very difficult to translate. Aphorism 46 reads: 'Das Wort "sein" bedeutet im Deutschen beides: Dasein und Ihmgehören.' (In *Hochzeitsvorbereitungen*, p. 44)

opportunities or possibilities of living, out of the reflected images of things. Everything in and about the castle is confusing and ambiguous in this way. Is it, in fact, a castle at all? It looks more like a rambling collection of low outhouses; its tower looks as though a madman had broken through the roof. What are we to 'make' of this? Everything we subsequently find out about its personnel and workings 'makes for' quite contradictory interpretations (as with the law-courts of *The Trial*). The castle officials are overworked night and day; yet Klamm himself sleeps most of the time. All the talk of tireless and efficient management is belied by the way documents are handled in the Village Superintendent's room or distributed amongst the officials at the inn. There is besides a grotesque lack of proportion between the size of this administrative apparatus and what is actually there to be administered. And there is a less comic, more disturbing lack of relationship between the supposedly superior intelligence of high-ranking officials and their coarse sexual demands, not to speak of the licence they permit in their underlings. Sex altogether 'means' something in the world of the castle of similar importance to its meaning in *The Trial*. But to be aware of its importance within this context does not make it any easier to say what its meaning is in words not taken from Kafka's actual text.

The problem of interpretation raised by *The Castle*, then, is ultimately insoluble because the thing itself has contradictory characteristics. Kafka's lucidity and genius lie in his allowing us to see that they are contradictory – which is to say, that the thing itself is self-contradictory. To say that the thing itself is 'life' or 'mind' will not do, because any such single interpretation implies that we have a larger frame of reference within which what is life and what is mind can be clearly located and related. Kafka has no such frame of reference. What he represents is the totally ambiguous character that existence takes on in these circumstances. My body alone, not to speak of the vaster physical universe beyond myself, is a tirelessly over-

administered nervous organism – messages hurrying to and
fro, cells endlessly having to be replaced, appetites sordidly to
be satisfied . . . And yet the mind itself mostly sleeps, while the
self can never be sure that it is wanted here. Do I possess my
body, or my body me? Who or what is struggling with whom
or what for recognition in this unidentifiable place? All that I
can be sure of is the wanting and the struggle. Thus, it is not
only impossible to interpret, say, the Assistants in this novel; it
is not even necessary to interpret them in order to see what sort
of role they play.

The role is very similar to that played by the warders, and
later by the executioners, in *The Trial*. K. is told that they have
been assigned to him, but he tries to disown them, complains
about them, ill-treats them, gets a stick ready to beat them, and
briefly drives them away – only to find that one of them has
won Frieda's sympathy and perhaps usurped his place with her.
It is tempting to interpret them here again as representing 'the
body' (intended not so much to assist K., for the body generally
seems to assist the rational self very little, but at least to cheer
him up, and win a bit of feminine sympathy besides). But any
close reading of Kafka's text will reveal that this kind of interpretation steps outside it, leaving behind quite inexplicable
details – as, for instance, why the assistants should be perched
on the bar *watching* K. who has been making love to Frieda. In
the closed world of *The Castle* we cannot say what is bodily and
what is spiritual, indeed nothing possesses one of these qualities
to the exclusion of the other; everything rather is ambiguously
compounded of both. But so, from Kafka's point of view, is
life, and it is a confusion arising from the use of language (and
of thought) to suppose that we can make such distinctions.

## Guilt and defiance

For Kafka, something worse than confusion and ambiguity
resulted from the mind's perverse efforts to rise above its
mortal condition. To question and resist the conventional 'pro-

cesses' of existence, as K. does in *The Trial* and Amalia does in
this novel, involves an apparently fatal guilt. K. is also guilty in
*The Castle* because (to quote from the protocol drawn up by
the Village Secretary): 'It was clear that the Land Surveyor did
not love Frieda. . . . It was simply out of calculation of the
vilest kind that K. made up to Frieda and stuck to her so long
as he still had hope that his plans would succeed.' Here, in a
few words, is the core of the plot, of which Amalia's story is a
variant. What the two stories have in common, apart from a
biographical foundation in Kafka's life (for his favourite sister,
Ottla, had resisted the family convention as he had done), is
that both K. and Amalia defy the castle, Amalia disinterestedly,
K. in a more devious manner involving other people. The in-
clusion of Amalia's story, and its similarity to K.'s, suggests
that the guilt involved is not of any conventional moral kind;
the circumstances in which K. finds himself make it almost
absurd to judge his behaviour by standards valid for any real
social situation. K. is guilty not because of the way he actually
treats Frieda – he is ready, after all, to marry her – but because
he is interested in her for the wrong reason.

The protocol quoted above gives one description – which
Kafka later deleted from the text – of K.'s 'wrong'. It does not
appear to be a very accurate description, in fact, if we compare
the word 'calculation' with what is described earlier as actually
happening when K. and Frieda first meet. 'Calculation'
describes better the protocol itself, and indeed all K.'s subse-
quent efforts to work out where he stands. It was this activity
which Kafka considered wrong and impossible of success. It
was to him a setting of himself over against life, opposite to it
and therefore outside it. And what he meant by 'life' was primarily his own inward awareness of it, so that this opposition
was a quite solitary struggle of himself with himself. 'O to be
opposite myself alone,' he exclaims in his diary, and describes
this wish as a desire 'for solitude beyond all consciousness of
anything else' (*nach besinnungsloser Einsamkeit*). K. and Klamm

are ultimately the same 'person', therefore: the vain pursuit by the self of itself as though it were something other, 'out there', to be possessed. Women, not as persons, but as sexual experiences, seem to offer K. access to this 'unconscious' goal, and to the extent to which Frieda or Pepi are realistic persons, he doubtless treats them wrongly. But the wrong that K. incurs is to be thought of not so much in moral terms as in metaphysical ones.

The sense of guilt, the wrong, that inspires Kafka's fiction derives not from any injustices he saw being perpetrated in society – though these he saw too and held views about them like many another socially responsible citizen – but from his self-observation as a writer, a thinker, a user of words. The wrong that he saw 'man' (if K.'s world is meant to represent a generalization of Kafka's experiences) perpetrating in this context was that man already *is* the thing that he tries to lay hold of, conquer, and justify as *his* through knowledge. He runs the risk, certainly, of destroying the thing he already has and is, his life, in his vain intellectual efforts to penetrate its mystery. But the damage he will do will be 'merely' psychological, as Amalia's parallel story shows.

All the Barnabas family needs to do is to stop worrying; they only cannot obtain pardon from the world because no offence has been committed by Amalia's refusal of life's impersonal demand for sexual perpetuation. They are guilty only of feeling guilt. Amalia herself evidently feels none and is content to live selflessly in the village. Above all she is capable of feeling no doubt and no curiosity about her position. She talks with no one about it, and no one talks to her. K. cannot be satisfied with any such silent state of being. He is for ever interrogating the world, and cannot settle quietly in the village, not only because it is so 'low-browed' (a visual symbol of its mindless state) but simply because: 'It would say nothing to me.' The German phrase he uses is the idiom: *Es würde mir nicht zusagen,* which in English has to be translated as: 'It would not suit me.' But the English idiom, deriving from a quite different philological root meaning 'to follow', fails to remind us of the state of confrontation, opposition, and exclusion which for Kafka explained why the world can never 'suit' the thinking mind. Life 'speaks' to the writer largely because he opposes and will not quietly take his place in it.

# 4

# Conclusion:
# The Problem of Interpretation

It may seem perhaps superfluous to insist on a conclusion, dealing with the problem of interpreting Kafka, when this entire study has from the beginning been concerned with just this question. Kafka himself writes about nothing else; all his works are essays in the problem of interpretation. As we have seen, he presents his readers with a single, but usually also weird situation, and then explores its significance, partly by actions resembling (not very closely) what in more conventional literature constitutes the story or plot, but mainly by speculative discussions of great length, subtlety, and lucidity – which get absolutely nowhere. No advance in 'positive' understanding is made, and the working out of the initial situation is on the verge of appearing (and perhaps will appear to later generations of readers) as exceedingly tiresome and negative. That is why a case can be made for rating Kafka's short stories as superior works of art, more likely to endure as masterpieces than the novels that have recently enjoyed most fame. One suspects that the fame of his longer fiction is partly due to its providing a gymnasium for the favourite pastime of modern thinkers – especially academic ones, and without the contemporary enthusiasm for literary criticism as a means of education, Kafka would not have become as famous as he is – which is to exercise the intellect with much personal earnestness and little public relevance. This suspicion brings us back, however, to the more fundamental question raised at the outset: how has it come about that an author who was himself so apparently indifferent to the world about him should have produced stories that have enjoyed a serious claim to be considered as the most relevant myths of the modern age?

Several of Kafka's stories deal quite explicitly with the subject of the individual's relationship to the community, of private interpretations to public life, and it will be appropriate to look at them here. They are: *Beim Bau der chinesischen Mauer* (1917, 'The Chinese Wall'), *Forschungen eines Hundes* (1922, 'Investigations of a Dog'), and *Josefine, die Sängerin oder Das Volk der Mäuse* (1924, 'Josephine, the Singer, or The Mouse People'). 'The Investigations of a Dog' is particularly interesting in this connection, because it tells of a lifetime of solemn research 'into the simplest questions', and describes how the arduous process of research has not led to any scientific conclusion – the narrator is, he says, 'incapable of science' in the normal sense, and persists in the name of a higher 'ultimate science, prizing freedom above everything else' – but how it has led him to something quite different, namely, an ecstatic vision of a dog who sings. He never actually finds the answer to his question, 'what the canine race nourishes itself on', but he does experience music again, which was what made him ask his question in the first place. The visionary scene at the end harks back to a remembered occasion in childhood, when the narrator saw a troupe of performing dogs (just as Kafka had been impressed by the troupe of Yiddish actors) and was overwhelmed 'by their courage in facing so openly the music of their own making'. These dogs not only made music but stood upon their hind legs, 'as if nature were an error', and caused the narrator to feel that 'the world was standing on its head'. In other words, the mystery of what art is, and the overwhelming effect that beauty has on us, prompts other, 'simple' questions about the way we live, and what we are 'nourished' on.

Now, these basic questions, whose answer the community takes for granted, and which are bound up with the oldest moral codes and religious rituals of the race, are of a kind that scientific research cannot possibly answer. The greater part of this story is taken up with discussion of the problems involved in 'research'. The investigating dog, as a result of his persistent inquiries, has 'felt outlawed in my innermost heart and run my head against the traditional walls of my species like a savage'. He has 'asked no assistance from the dog community, and indeed rejected it in the most determined manner'. This does not mean, however, that he does not care about his fellow-creatures; on the contrary, 'all that I cared about was the race of dogs, that and nothing else. For what is there actually except our own species?' This question points to the moral – or something more fundamental even than morality – as well as to the quiet humour of this story. For the reader knows that there are men as well as dogs, and that all these solemn mysteries about where dogs' food comes from are merely a dog's way of describing the (to him) inexplicable dishing out of nourishment 'from above' by human beings.

As with all fables, however, this translation of the story to another level only confronts us again with the same problem in another form. What are human beings nourished on? By bread alone? And here again the fundamental assumption of the questioner is of crucial importance: 'What is there actually except our own species? To whom else can one appeal in the wide and empty world?' Kafka then describes the predicament of the modern mind as it tries to make sense of its condition without appeal to anyone else:

> All knowledge, the totality of all questions and answers, is contained in the dog. If one could but realize this knowledge, if one could but bring it into the light of day, if we dogs would but own that we know infinitely more than we admit to ourselves . . . But the one thing that you long to win above all, the admission of knowledge remains denied to you. To such prayers, whether silent or loud, the only answer you get, even after you have employed your

powers of seduction to the utmost, are vacant stares, averted glances, troubled and veiled eyes.
(*Forschungen eines Hundes*, in *Beschreibung eines Kampfes*, p. 255)

The narrator then goes on to ponder on the still greater mystery that, after all, he himself is a dog, and the answer he seeks as to the nature of dogdom is contained within himself. This gives him a feeling of solidarity with his fellow-dogs: 'You also have the dog knowledge; well, bring it out, not merely in the form of a question, but as an answer. The great choir of dogdom will join in as if it had been waiting for you. Then you will have clarity, truth, avowal, as much as you desire. The roof of this wretched life, of which you say so many hard things, will burst open, and all of us shoulder to shoulder, will ascend into the lofty realm of freedom.' Kafka perceives, however, that this ideal of solidarity – which reflects his own renewed interest in the last years of his life in Zionism and the Jewish faith – is false. While he admits that the knowledge he desires, 'and the key to it as well', he cannot possess 'except in common with all the others, I cannot grasp it without their help', he has to admit also that: 'If I remain faithful to a metaphor, then the goal of my aims, my questions, my enquiries, appears monstrous.' For the enthusiasm he feels for collective solidarity amongst his people, which will make manifest the secret embodied in their bones, does not express any genuine readiness to join them. What he would really do is to dismiss them utterly, 'to the ordinary life they love', and to remain himself quite alone, feeding on the marrow of his entire race.

The metaphor expresses vividly Kafka's guilty sense of being a parasite as a writer, and he makes his judgement doubly clear when he concludes: 'The marrow that I am discussing here is no food; on the contrary, it is poison.' He cannot commune with his neighbour, even though he knows that every dog must in some degree 'have like me the impulse to question', indeed, 'it is the peculiarity of dogs to be always asking questions'. But

they ask them 'confusedly all together; it is as if in doing that
they were trying to obliterate every trace of the genuine questions'. The genuine questions are asked by himself alone, and
he pursues them with a passion akin to that of a 'scientist'. This
does not mean that he thinks of his research as a material
science * (for which he has an 'instinctive' incapacity); his inquiry has the spiritual seriousness of religious tradition, to
which he also feels himself to be rather superior, for he looks
down on his own generation of dogs as being in a state of
spiritual decline. He looks back nostalgically to the earlier
period of his race:

> Dogs had not yet become so doggish as today, the edifice
> was still loosely put together, the true Word could still
> have intervened, planning or replanning the structure,
> changing it at will, transforming it into its opposite; and
> the Word was there, was very near at least, on the tip of
> everybody's tongue, anyone might have hit upon it. And
> what has become of it today? Today one may pluck out
> one's very heart and not find it.          (ibid., p. 268)

It should now be becoming fairly clear what kind of 'research' the narrator is engaged in, and what kind of interpretation he is making of his canine culture in decline and of his own
place in it. It is a kind of interpretation that lies between – and
even pretends to combine – pure science and religious prophecy; it investigates simple but fundamental questions, draw-
ing its primary evidence and inspiration from the experience of
art. This manner of thinking about metaphysical and moral
questions in social, historical, and cultural terms may be said
to be typically German. It derives from the idealist metaphysics
of Hegel, Schopenhauer, and Nietzsche; by Kafka's time it had
permeated the minds of the most diverse thinkers, from Freud
to Spengler. He himself might have picked it up from reading

---

* The German word *Wissenschaft* does not have the same connotations
as the English word 'science', which refers almost exclusively to the natural
or empirical sciences. *Wissenschaft* refers to learning in the humane, as
well as in the pure, sciences.

Hegel's protesting disciple, Kierkegaard, or from contact with almost any of the cultural pessimists of his age, which is to say, almost any of his intelligent contemporaries. For it had taken hold of the spiritual life of Europe like a fever; indeed, the oppressive mood of cultural self-consciousness that it induced seemed particularly conducive to creative thought. While its home was Germany and central Europe, many French intellectuals were seduced by it (and since then still more have been); it spread as far as Spain in the writings of an Ortega y Gasset, and echoed in the Hegelian foundations of Marxism. Perhaps England and Italy have proved most resistant to it, but the academic world of America has fostered it in many later varieties. As a form of intellectual critique of life's meaning and civilization's value, it speaks with an authority that is devastatingly negative, for it is founded neither on faith nor on fact but on the unassailable ground of psychological analysis. Kafka's distinctive virtue as a writer in this tradition consists in his ability to render visible, in symbolic form, the way this type of thinking operates. He lays bare the state of mind, the motivation, and the attitudes on which its interpretation of the world is based. The symbolism Kafka uses to do this is graphic and lucid: the dog fasts, abstains totally from the food whose secret he is determined to have.

Kafka is more critical of the cultural critic's position than most writers have been. He keeps his feet on the ground as the 'hovering dogs', whom we may imagine to be his more highfalutin intellectual contemporaries, have not done. He has never actually seen them hover; he has seen dogs get two of their feet off the ground, but not all four. Such an existence would be entirely senseless in his view, but not for that reason not worth investigating. On the contrary, 'the most senseless seemed to me in this senseless world more probable than the sensible, and moreover particularly fertile for investigation'. The sentence sounds like a garbled pronouncement by Aristotle on art, and later the narrator tells us that 'someone now and then refers to art and artists' to explain these hovering creatures, who have 'no relation whatever to the life of the community'. That they are intellectuals of some sort seems clear enough from the fact that 'they are perpetually talking, partly of their philosophical reflections with which, seeing that they have completely renounced bodily exertion, they can continuously occupy themselves, partly of the observations they have made from their exalted stations'. This almost 'unendurable volubility' is to be explained, the narrator thinks, by their need to obtain pardon for their unjustifiable way of life; and here the criticism implicit in the gentle irony of the text would seem to extend to Kafka himself, who was always guiltily doubtful about the value of his activity as a writer. His research into this question has led him to the entirely negative conclusion that the only thing research can clarify is falsehood:

> The truth can never be discovered by such means – never can that stage be reached – but they [inquiries of this kind] throw light on some of the profounder ramifications of falsehood. For all the senseless phenomena of our existence, and the most senseless most of all, are susceptible of investigation. (ibid., p. 262)

This, too, might be a description of Kafka's own writings: an investigation of the senseless, a clarification of what is not the truth. As we shall see presently, the value of this strange exercise is to expose the way in which the interpretative intelligence works. This can only be grasped negatively, in isolation from the world.

'Investigations of a Dog' exposes, then, the psychology of the modern critical intelligence, driving itself to total abstinence from life, in both a physical and material sense, totally committed to an utterly wearisome task, 'but for that very reason resolved to pursue it indefatigably . . . so as to be left free to regain the ordinary, calm, happy life of everyday'. That the narrator will never regain it is obvious from the way the story is told as a parable about dogs. But the (human) reader is released by the symbolism from the dog's delusions, and thus indirectly raised up above the typical 'delusions' of the modern mind. One by one, the great themes of modern literature and thought are rehearsed. This dog has had some tremendous aesthetic experience when young which determined his fate, 'making me feel sorry for myself; it robbed me of my childhood . . . but perhaps I have the prospect of far more childish happiness, earned by a life of hard work, in my old age than any actual child'. Might we not think of Proust trying to recapture the lost paradise of his early years? Then we find Kafka's dog obsessed with the limits of language, the futility of expression, and the menacing challenge of silence. 'I only want to be stimulated by the silence which rises up around me as the ultimate answer . . . We survive all questions, even our own, bulwarks of silence that we are.' Might not Beckett have spoken thus? And when the strange hound appears at the end, 'not at all extraordinary' in himself, but transfigured in the delirious gaze of the narrator who is lying in the blood he has vomited, we think inevitably of Kafka himself, and of the piercing, monotonous, unendurable note of 'music' that the most ordinary existence, indeed the mere fact of existence, emitted 'solely for my sake' when he was, as the dog puts it here, 'quite beyond myself' (*außer mir*). But we might think equally of other modern, and especially German, writers who have attained this mystical awareness of reality as something unbearably terrible and beautiful – writers like Nietzsche and Rilke. And finally, there is the basic theme of the story, so fundamental to this and all Kafka's work that we might overlook it as a cliché of modern literature altogether: the solitary hero, set in opposition to all the world, who asks a question of metaphysical importance that his society cannot answer. But this story, like the other two we shall briefly look at here, puts this familiar modern motif in a new light.

The ironically metaphysical question about the provenance of dog's food that obsesses the narrator – a question which was originally inspired, as we saw, by an overwhelming artistic experience – not only sets him apart from the rest of his race, making him feel prematurely alone so that he loses his childhood; it also gives him a peculiar power of perception as regards his fellow-beings. He begins to see everything that they do as inadequate, and their very appearance as disgusting. Even though he knows that it is in their nature to ask questions, he finds their questions and their answers, which 'enable them to bear this life', to be inauthentic, evasions rather than confrontations. The narrator declares that the 'burden of my complaint, the kernel of it', is summed up in the doubt whether he has any 'real colleagues', or 'real *comrades*', as he sometimes puts it. What prevents him from believing 'that all dogs from the beginning of time have been my colleagues, all diligent in their own way, all unsuccessful in their own way, all silent or falsely garrulous in their own way, as hopeless research is apt to make one'? The only answer that follows is the reflection that his whole life of solitary investigation would in that case have been a waste of time: 'But in that case I need not have severed myself from my fellows at all, I could have remained quietly among the others, I had no need to fight my way out like a stubborn child through the closed ranks of the grown ups.' Kafka touches here on the critical problem of modern society, the crisis that has caused classes, races, groups, and generations to tear one another apart. And we touch here in Kafka's work the point of discovery that enabled him, despite all his preoccupation with seemingly private and psychological problems to create myths that embody so much of twentieth-century man's most disastrous experience. Kafka needed only to study his neighbour, like the dog in this story, needed only to reflect upon the relationship that existed between himself and his father, or between himself as a person in society and himself as a thinking, solitary mind, to perceive the motivations that would drive others to torture, deceive, and destroy themselves – and not just in imagination, but in reality.

The differences that separate the narrator from his fellows are all matters of convention. In his first encounter with the musical dogs as a child, it is he who is appalled, not they, by what they are doing, he who is amazed at their 'courage in facing so openly the music of their own making', and morally shaken that they should expose themselves in this un-doggy way. It is he who breaks out of the 'labyrinth of wooden bars' that should have kept him in his place (as conventions are meant to do), to confront these artists with protests about the enormity of their performance, about which they seem so unconcerned, being totally absorbed (as artists generally are) by the technical difficulties of their art. Later, when he considers discussing with his neighbour the questions that are obsessing him, he desists simply because he knows 'what course the conversation would take. He would . . . agree – agreement is the best weapon of defence – and the matter would be buried.' It is his neighbour's, his people's ability to bear without worrying these basic questions, to accept them as answers, as 'agreements', rather than as questions, that 'fills me with dejection and confuses me', so the narrator tells us. 'Their belief that it is simple prevents further enquiry.' And when finally the narrator, in his inability to accept that 'it' is simple, embarks upon his unheard-of course of inquiry by fasting, he breaks the unwritten law – and what else is convention? – of his race. The vision with which he is rewarded is quite literally a creation, a projection (in psychological terms) of his spiritual hunger. 'In the midst of pain I felt a longing to go on fasting, and I followed it as greedily as if it were a strange dog.' This is then exactly what appears to him in his fainting state: a strange dog. No analysis could be more exact of the way in which Kafka's creative imagination responded to the world. It happens also to be a prophetic description of the spiritual hunger and hallucinations of the modern age.

The almost automatic assumption of Europe's intelligentsia for the last century or more has been that the conventional

values or 'agreements' of society are false. This habit of mind
has grown amongst aspirant intellectuals at an ever-younger
age and on an ever-increasing scale. Kafka was by no means
the first writer to anticipate and express it; but he remains
remarkable for his ability to rise above and reflect upon this
mental attitude, not taking its criticisms of the world literally,
that is, as if it showed what was really 'wrong' in some still conventional sense, but showing instead how questionable this way
of thinking in itself is. The criticism of the world inspired by
such metaphysical uncertainty cannot be proved on purely
objective grounds; what is seen in the world is a reflection of
the viewer's state of mind. The collapse of convention, that
cliché of contemporary thought, is a psychological collapse,
rather than something that has happened 'out there' in society.
Or rather, Kafka teaches us to see that the ultimate terror
brought about by such a collapse is that we feel trapped inside
a deluded consciousness of the world, regarding *all* conventional representations of existence as false, but for that very
reason unable to extricate ourselves from them. Kafka's
mythology makes us aware of the impossibility of distinguish-
ing between what happens 'out there' and our consciousness of
it. This is like living in a nightmare, knowing it to be a nightmare, but being unable to wake up. Kafka's myths illustrate
the psychological pattern of the urges that move men in this
spiritual situation: the revolutionary urge to break the illusions
of convention, contempt for the scruffy, conformist neighbour,
who accepts the dream as true, and desire for a nobler solidarity
of the race and a higher type of individual. The fantasies of the
dog in this story, who dreams of ascending shoulder to shoulder
into freedom and who hears in his sick despair a sublime
transcendent voice, are the product of the same imagination
that is disgusted by his bourgeois neighbour and outraged by
the moral inadequacies of his society.

A similar psychological pattern underlies the story 'The
Great Wall of China'. The narrator is again a scholarly in-

vestigator set apart from his people, who for him are guilty of 'a certain feebleness of faith and imaginative power'. In the end he desists from further research because 'to set about establishing a fundamental defect here would mean undermining not only our consciences, but, what is worse, our feet'. In studying the great wall that everyone believes to protect the empire, he alone has sought for 'an explanation of the system of piecemeal construction that goes farther than the one that contented people then'. In the early days, people had not meditated on the mystery of the wall's construction, which is so obviously inexpedient since it consists of as many gaps as ramparts, because they were content with a maxim that assumed human thought must correspond to nature, the order of meaning to the order of the world, and science to the law of God. The narrator stands above all earlier beliefs about the wall, especially those of a religious character; for him 'no lightning flashes any longer from the long-since vanished thunder clouds'. But he comes to a kind of religious conclusion nevertheless, though it is founded on different grounds now. He believes there must always have been a 'high command'; the conventions of the world cannot be regarded as merely secular, sociological arrangements. That the wall – of human achievement, perhaps in a metaphorical sense, of knowledge – is so full of holes is to be explained by the psychological wisdom of the 'high command':

> Human nature, essentially changeable, unstable as the dust, can endure no restraint; if it binds itself it soon begins to tear madly at its bonds, until it rends everything asunder, the wall, the bonds and its very self.
>
> (*Beim Bau der chinesischen Mauer*,
> in *Beschreibungen eines Kampfes*, p. 72)

The result of this subjectively wise, even if objectively crazy, method of construction is to prevent any such outbreak of destructive despair and to preserve feelings of the greatest solidarity amongst the people. They labour on, confident that 'every fellow country-man was a brother for whom one was

building a wall of protection . . . Unity! Unity! Shoulder to
shoulder, a ring of brothers, a current of blood no longer con-
fined within the narrow circulation of one body, but sweetly
rolling and yet ever returning throughout the endless leagues of
China.'

As we recognize the same pattern of events and responses in
'The Great Wall of China' that we have seen in so many of
Kafka's stories and novels, we can begin to sum up the problem
of interpretation that they present. Kafka *might* be writing here
of a political 'high command', which understands the psychological needs of its citizens so well that it can produce a state of
popular national brotherhood by cunningly manipulating the
economy while leaving the people in ignorance. (Later in the
story the extent of this ignorance is made quite plain.) Or
Kafka *might* even here be thought of – as he has been thought
of in connection with his major works – as writing about God,
the structure of Creation, and the part played in it by human
beings. As he describes the problem posed by the vastness and
uniqueness of this edifice, and of 'the many legends to which
the building of the wall gave rise, which cannot be verified, at
least by any man with his own eyes and judgement, on account
of the extent of the structure', Kafka *might* be taking up in his
own picturesque language a problem that has exercised philosophers and theologians: namely, by what standards can human
beings judge metaphysical questions concerning the whole universe, of which they are a mere subordinate part and outside
which they have nothing to judge it by. On the other hand,
Kafka *might* well be writing metaphorically about something
rather different, as we have already hinted. The story could be
about the piecemeal character of human learning, which is to
say, of thinking and writing. Words themselves, which can be
built into coherent stretches of 'wall', or sentences, leave huge
holes and gaps between one and the next, and cannot ever
protect us fully against the menace of reality. Sometimes, of
course, in the enthusiasm of building some small piece of wall,

a few impressive sentences, a poem perhaps, or a story, a writer may produce in all his being, and in his hearers too, a sense of 'Unity! Unity!' A surge of meaningful feelings unites the words in the sentence – or equally we might say, unites the readers of the poem; we are, after all, taking Kafka's story in a metaphorical sense, way beyond its literal meaning, and who shall say what is the 'right' meaning of a word? Language itself gives rise to legends 'which cannot be verified, on account of the extent of the structure'. Kafka *might* simply be telling a literal story about the Great Wall of China, and who shall say that this is not interesting enough as it stands? Why do we have to interpret it? Why don't we just read it?

Exactly the same question can be asked, of course, about life itself. Why don't we just live it? The answer is that it seems to be saying something to us. The situation is summed up for us in the parable told in the second half of 'The Great Wall of China'. The Emperor has sent a message to you, the humble subject, from the centre of the world; but the messenger cannot get through, the clutter and refuse and sheer 'overpopulation' of existence prevent him from reaching you. So 'you sit at your window when evening falls and dream it to yourself'. In the passages before and after this beautiful parable, Kafka plays with the idea that the Emperor is really dead, but that this makes no difference to what the people dream; the Empire itself goes on, indeed, it is 'immortal'. To the detached observer there is no rational connection, no true correspondence, between what the people believe and what the case is. But it makes no difference, life goes on, indeed 'it' is immortal. Only one thing might seriously threaten it, 'undermine our consciences and what is worse our feet' (that is, our real ability to 'stand' it at all), and that would be to discover the truth, or rather the total absence of it, the lack of any possibility of it, in all human endeavour. And so the inquirer, the author, desists from further inquiry. Did Kafka, then, desist, and should we likewise not persist? The paradox of this intellectual situation is that he and

we could only do this by either not beginning at all, or destroying everything at the end, or – if a third alternative is permissible – by writing in such a way that what is written both
means something and means nothing at one and the same time.
And this, as we remarked at the outset, was Kafka's extraordinary intellectual project. When he was in a mood to believe
that in much of his writing he had not succeeded, he fell back in
despair on the second alternative, and asked that it should be
destroyed.

Kafka's strangely symbolic fiction, which presents so obvious
a challenge to interpretation, resembles real life to the extent to
which living too is felt to present a similar challenge. What
Kafka is 'imitating', in the same way that all artists may be said
to be making a likeness or copy of something real, is the
experience of this challenge. He is not representing the world
according to the rules of some convention that purports to tell
us what it means; he is representing the process of describing
the world when no convention is available to tell us what it
means, not even a convention that will enable us to distinguish
what is there from what we think is there. In such a situation of
profound spiritual doubt, Kafka certainly does not provide *an*
interpretation of the world, and criticism cannot consequently
provide *an* interpretation of Kafka's work. What he provides is
an image of how experience looks when all interpretations are
called in doubt. He does not write simple-minded existentialist
literature of the kind that supposedly exposes the artificiality of
human values, psychic structures, language games, and the like;
Kafka is too desperately – and humorously – aware of the
absurdity in the claims of any mind that judges everything to
be absurd. What standard is it judging by? Where does it
stand? Kafka's writing is directed against the absurdity not of
the world, but of writing. It reflects its own activity, its own
reality – and utter artificiality. The fact that the resulting symbolism bears some resemblance to events in the outside world
tells us less about those events than about the way we are in the

habit (perhaps) of thinking about them. If we have no social or political conventions we really believe in, if we have no faith in any value more positive than to gaze without bias or commitment upon the truth, then the truth will become a nightmare.

Many writers, and amongst them some of the greatest, like Dante, and Shakespeare, and Goethe, have recognized the limits of what writing may achieve in the face of life's mystery – and death's. But none has described these limits more modestly or wittily than Kafka in 'Josephine, the Singer'. The story forms a contrast and companion piece to 'The Burrow', and in it Kafka reveals the secret of his art's success, instead of its hopeless failure. But his ironical aesthetic theory makes success and failure ultimately indistinguishable. For the singer, he says, cannot actually sing any better than other people; if anything, Josephine sings rather worse. The only difference made by art is that it is a self-conscious and deliberate imitation of what everyone else does spontaneously.

> To crack a nut is certainly not an art, therefore no one would dare to bring an audience together and crack nuts before them in order to entertain them. But if someone should do this nevertheless, and if he successfully accomplishes his 'art', then the thing does cease to be a mere nutcracking. Or rather, it continues to be still a matter of cracking nuts, but it becomes apparent that we have normally overlooked what an art this was, because we could do it so easily, and that this new nutcracker was the first person to show us what the real nature of the business was; and it might then even be more effective if he was a little less good at cracking nuts than the majority of us.
>
> (In *Erzählungen*, pp. 270 f)

# Bibliography

GERMAN EDITIONS

*Gesammelte Werke*, ed. M. Brod, 2nd edn, New York/Frankfurt am Main: *Der Prozeß*, 1950; *Das Schloß*, 1951; *Tagebücher 1910–1923*, 1951; *Briefe an Milena*, ed. W. Haas, 1952; *Erzählungen*, 1952; *Amerika*, 1953; *Hochzeitsvorbereitungen auf dem Lande und andere Prosa aus dem Nachlaß*, 1953; *Beschreibung eines Kampfes. Novellen, Skizzen, Aphorismen aus dem Nachlaß*, 1954; *Briefe 1902–1924*, 1958.

*Sämtliche Erzählungen*, ed. P. Raabe, Frankfurt am Main, 1970.

*Briefe an Felice und andere Korrespondenz*, ed. and introd. E. Heller, Frankfurt am Main, 1967.

ENGLISH EDITIONS

*The Castle*, tr. W. and E. Muir, 1930; rev. edn, 1953.

*The Great Wall of China and Other Pieces*, tr. E. and W. Muir, 1933.

*The Trial*, tr. W. and E. Muir, 1937; rev. edn, 1955.

*The Metamorphosis*, tr. A. L. Lloyd, 1937.

*America*, tr. W. and E. Muir, 1938.

*The Penal Colony: Stories and short pieces*, tr. W. and E. Muir, 1948.

*The Diaries of Franz Kafka*, tr. J. Kresh, 2 vols, 1948–9.

*Letters to Milena*, tr. J. and T. Stern, 1953.

*Wedding Preparations in the Country, and other posthumous prose writings*, tr. E. Kaiser and E. Wilkins, 1954.

*Metamorphosis and other stories*, tr. E. and W. Muir, 1961 (Penguin).

WRITINGS ON KAFKA

(*In German*)

H. Järv, *Die Kafka Literatur*, Malmö–Lund, 1961.

M. Brod, *Über Franz Kafka*, Frankfurt am Main, 1966.

W. Emrich, *Franz Kafka*, Bonn, 1958.

W. H. Sokel, *Franz Kafka. Tragik und Ironie*, Munich, 1964.

K. Wagenbach, *Franz Kafka. Eine Biographie seiner Jugend*, Bern, 1958.

*(In English)*

G. Anders, *Franz Kafka*, London, 1960.

A. Flores and H. Swander, eds., *Franz Kafka Today*, Madison, 1958.

R. D. Gray, *Kafka's Castle*, Cambridge, 1956.

R. D. Gray, ed., *Kafka: A Collection of Critical Essays*, Englewood Cliffs, 1962.

H. Politzer, *Franz Kafka. Parable and Paradox*, New York, rev. edn 1966.